A
MOTCOMBE
MISCELLANY

Laurence Clark

First published in the United Kingdom in 2012
by The Hobnob Press, PO Box 1838, East Knoyle, Salisbury, SP3 6FA
www.hobnobpress.co.uk

British Library Cataloguing in Publication Data
A catalogue record for this book is available from the British Library

ISBN 978-1-906978-07-5

Typeset in Scala 11/12.5 pt. Typesetting and origination by John Chandler
Printed by Lightning Source

Contents

CONTENTS

Preface

THIS book contains articles written by myself for the *Dorset Year Book* and the *Villager* over a period of twenty years. They have mostly been on Motcombe and its past including residents who, in their various ways, have contributed to the life of this village. Because of this certain themes recur at different points in the book, and readers will discover some repetition.

I was born and grew up in Motcombe. Although not now a resident I have always maintained a close connection with my native village where members of my family still live and have done so for several generations.

The purpose of this book is to reach a wider readership so that the knowledge that I have gained over many years on this North Dorset village can be passed on 'before the sunset fades'.

Laurence Clark

I

The Grosvenor Family

Elizabeth Mary Marchioness of Westminster
1797–1891

A GRAVE of particular interest in Motcombe churchyard is that of Elizabeth Mary, Marchioness of Westminster who was the widow of Richard, the second Marquess and mother of Hugh, the first Duke of Westminster. One would have supposed that she would have been buried beside her husband, to whom she had been happily married for fifty years, in the family graveyard at Eccleston, near Eaton Hall, the Grosvenors' seat in Cheshire, but a memorial on the north wall of Motcombe Church, erected by her youngest daughter, Lady Theodora Guest, states that she was

> . . . buried by her desire amongst her own people . . . in the churchyard at Motcombe.

Lady Elizabeth and her husband had first become acquainted with Motcombe sixty years previously, when as Lord and Lady Belgrave, they visited Motcombe House, which had been given to them by Earl Grosvenor, Belgrave's father, as a country home of their own. Later that year, Earl Grosvenor was created first Marquess of Westminster and the Belgraves became Earl and Countess Grosvenor. Motcombe House, which had hitherto been called 'Palmer's Place', was on the Motcombe Estate, one of the properties in North Dorset, including the town of Shaftesbury and the Manor of Gillingham, which Earl Grosvenor had bought in the 1820s. This was the old Motcombe House, which was pulled down when the present building, now Port Regis School, was built in 1893. Lady Elizabeth loved her new home and the beautiful countryside around; for Motcombe in those days was a pretty village with thatched cottages and farmhouses surrounded by trees and abounding in apple orchards. Her affection for the village was extended into affection for its people which continued throughout her long life.

Even after her husband had succeeded to the Marquisate in 1845, on the death of his father, thereby inheriting his immense wealth and vast estates, the modest-sized Motcombe House remained their favourite home in preference to the palatial Eaton Hall, and the stately Grosvenor House in London. Here they spent as much time as possible together with their large family. Lady Elizabeth had borne thirteen children, nine of whom, much to her great chagrin, were girls. One, Evelyn, died of typhus at Motcombe House, at the age of twelve. Of the boys, one died of infancy, and another, Gilbert, died aged twenty-one while serving in the Navy.

Dowager Marchioness of Westminster

Lady Elizabeth's affection for the people of Motcombe was demonstrated by her concern for their welfare and she was particularly interested in the education of the children. In 1839, she built a school next to the church. In 1874, a further building was added to serve as a separate school for the boys, while the original building continued as a school for girls and infants. They were appropriately called the Marchioness of Westminster's Schools. Both buildings are still in use today as Motcombe Church of England Primary School.

The Marchioness maintained her interest and financial support for the rest of her life. Her visits to the schools are recorded in the school log books and make interesting reading. An entry in June, 1882, reads:

> Lady Westminster gave a reading lesson to Standard III and said they read very nicely.

This is the last time she appears to have taken a lesson, but she was then in her eighty-fifth year. Thereafter, she confined herself to inspecting and commenting on the children's work, as evidenced by an entry dated 10 July, 1885:

> Visited by Lady Westminster who was well pleased with the needlework and knitting.

Her last visit was on 4 June, 1886. Then in her eighty-ninth year, she was accompanied by her beloved granddaughter, Elizabeth Guest, aged seven, the only child of Lady Theodora and Merthyr Guest.

When old age prevented her from visiting her schools, she continued to be present at the annual treat for the children held in the grounds of Motcombe House. She was remembered by one Motcombe schoolchild at that time as a little old lady dressed in black, who sat in a bath chair. It was the custom for the children to bring bunches of flowers and to give three cheers at the end of the occasion to mark their appreciation.

During his lifetime, her husband, Lord Westminster, was considered to be a model landlord, who carried out many improvements on his numerous estates, Motcombe being no exception. The village was extensively rebuilt, many of the old thatched cottages and some of the farms being pulled down and replaced by buildings, dating from the 1850s and 1860s, still surviving in Motcombe today. No fewer than twenty-two pairs of cottages were built, containing all the modern conveniences of that period, including three bedrooms so that parents, boys and girls could have separate rooms. A piped water supply was provided to conveniently positioned public tap houses. Later, after her husband's death, Lady Elizabeth herself financed the building of a reservoir. More pipes were then laid bringing water to most of the cottages and farms.

The personal attention that Lady Westminster gave to her schools was similarly bestowed on the cottagers. Acting like a present day social worker, she paid visits to their homes to see for herself how they were faring. Families found to be living in overcrowded conditions were rehoused in modern

Richard, 2nd Marquess of Westminster

Westminster cottages. One example is given of a large family moving into the village who were initially living in a small cottage totally lacking any conveniences. When this came to the attention of her ladyship, they were accommodated in a Westminster cottage. The mother of that family was for ever afterwards grateful to Lady Westminster for this good deed.

Motcombe was then, however, a closely knit community; most families were interrelated and they resented the arrival of strangers. The village cobbler decided that the children of this family, being outsiders, did not qualify for the new boots provided by Lady Westminster for poor children, which meant most of the village children, but on hearing this the noble lady decreed otherwise.

Despite free education, better housing and other provisions, the labourer's lot remained a hard one. Agricultural labourers' wages were abysmally low; absenteeism was high in Lady Westminster's schools, particularly among the boys who went 'bird-keeping' when only of tender years to provide a few pennies for hard-pressed households.

After the death of the Marquess in 1869, the bulk of the Westminster estates were inherited by Hugh, the elder son, who five years later was to be created the first Duke of Westminster. The Dowager Marchioness, who was bequeathed the Dorset estates for her lifetime, now held the Lordship of the Manor, a position she was to retain for the next twenty-two years. With the help and companionship of Lady Theodora, she continued her good works, providing further amenities and liberally supporting causes which benefited her people. But she was well able to afford to do so: despite the fact that her son had inherited the lion's share of the properties, the Marquess had left her a very wealthy woman. In 1871, she provided a site for the Westminster Memorial Hospital at Shaftesbury, which was built by public subscription, in memory of her husband. She also contributed £2,000 for the establishment of an endowment fund. The improvement in the water supply at Motcombe in 1872 and the building of the boys' school in 1874, which cost £520, have already been mentioned.

Semley and Todber Churches were rebuilt at her expense. She gave generously to the clothing clubs and contributed substantial amounts to church improvements and repairs, and, to benefit her own family, the stables at Motcombe House were rebuilt.

During the latter part of her life, a significant change took place in Lady Westminster's political outlook and attitudes. Traditionally the Grosvenor family had supported the Whigs and later the Liberals, her husband having been an M.P. for Chester for sixteen years and her two sons Liberal M.P.s until their elevation to the House of Lords. She had shared the same views as her husband and had taken a keen interest in politics. In old age, she veered sharply to the right, supporting the Conservatives, admiring Disraeli, and detesting Gladstone as did her friend, Queen Victoria, with whom she on occasions corresponded. When the Grand Old Man visited Gillingham and Shaftesbury in the 1880s, the Dowager Marchioness ordered the lodge keeper to close the gates on the Gillingham/Shaftesbury Road at the time he was due to pass, to mark her displeasure.

It had seemed that the old Marchioness would live to celebrate her centenary, but this was not to be; she died three days after here ninety-fourth birthday, nevertheless she had survived to extreme old age at a time when life expectancy was shorter than today.

The end came when she was staying with her daughter and son-in-law, Lady Theodora and Merthyr Guest at Inwood House, near Templecombe. Her body was brought back to Motcombe House on the day of the funeral. Although she had wished to be buried in a quiet an unostentatious manner, it was, in fact, a spectacular event, as no fewer than five hundred people took part in the procession, which was headed by the Mayor and Corporation of Shaftesbury, and over three thousand people lined the road to the church, which was packed to capacity. At the end of the service, the mourners processed to the flower-lined grave, where in accordance with her wishes, she was laid to rest amongst her Motcombe people. Of those filing past the grave, forty were schoolchildren from the village, each of whom deposited a bunch of flowers as a tribute to one who had always shown concern for their welfare. Lady Theodora received a personally signed letter of sympathy from Queen Victoria, who had constantly enquired about the Marchioness's condition during her final illness. Hugh, Duke of Westminster, claimed to be indisposed and did not attend his mother's funeral.

Dowager Marchioness of Westminster at the age of 92

Instead a memorial service was held in his private chapel at Eaton Hall. Amongst the numerous floral tributes was one inscribed 'From her loving grandchild, Goodie.' This was Elizabeth Guest, the little girl who had accompanied the Marchioness on her last visit to the village schools and who is now buried at the foot of her grandmother's grave.

The Motcombe and surrounding estates were inherited by her younger son, Richard, who had been created first Baron Stalbridge in 1886. He was succeeded on his death in 1912 by his son, Hugh, who sold the estates after the First World War. When Hugh died in 1949, the title became extinct, his only son having been killed in an aeroplane accident in Australia. Both the first and second Baron Stalbridge are buried in Motcombe churchyard.

From the Duke of Westminster, the line has continued, albeit indirectly, to the present holder of the title, who is the sixth Duke, and the Marchioness's great-great-grandson.

Her successor in Motcombe, Richard, Lord Stalbridge, proved to be a pleasant and conscientious landlord. Building a new Motcombe House in 1893, he endeavoured to continue in the manner established by his mother, but on account of financial problems was compelled to give up living at Motcombe House in 1905.

Due to her long association with Motcombe she had become an institution in the village, greatly liked and respected, despite her privileged position and affluence which contrasted with the deprivation and poverty around her. The poor had recognised that she had made genuine efforts to improve their lot and by her actions had shown that she had identified herself with their wellbeing. The Dowager Marchioness had demonstrated her preference for a simple country life when, years earlier, she had chosen Motcombe House as her main residence. She had a dislike of pomp and grandeur and had been highly critical of her son for accepting a dukedom, considering it an unnecessary and unwarranted ostentation.

Towards the end of her long life, she had shunned the company of most members of her large family, preferring just to be with Theodora and Merthyr and particularly enjoying the companionship of her little granddaughter 'Goody'. Her relationship with her two sons had become very strained and they in turn regarded her as being imperious, obstinate and difficult. It would be appropriate to end with the words of Canon Smith, Vicar of Motcombe, in a sermon preached at her funeral:

> Others could tell of her ancestral rank and her large possessions and her beneficent works, but those present could tell from personal knowledge of what gives rank its highest title of nobility – her great goodness of

heart and her one wish to use her possessions for the good of those amongst whom she lived.

A Family Feud

THE will of the Dowager Marchioness of Westminster, who died in 1891 at the advanced age of ninety-four, was the cause of a bitter feud in her family, which included her elder son the Duke of Westminster.

The quarrel arose because she had left the bulk of her considerable fortune to her youngest and favourite daughter Lady Theodora Guest, who had been her constant companion and support during her long widowhood and, by means of a codicil, she had increased her bequest to her son-in-law, Merthyr Guest, from ten thousand pounds to thirty thousand pounds. Again, by a codicil, she had reduced from ten thousand pounds to one thousand pounds the legacies to two of her daughters, Lady Agnes Frank and Lady Jane Lindsay, who were most in need of financial help. She also provided one thousand pounds each for three of her other five daughters, the Countess Macclesfield, the Dowager Lady Wenlock and Lady Leigh, but the Dowager Duchess of Northumberland and Lady Shaw-Stewart received nothing.

The Dowager had inherited her fortune, equivalent to several million pounds today, from her husband, the second Marquess of Westminster, who had also left her a life interest in his estates at Motcombe, Shaftesbury, Stalbridge and Fonthill in Wiltshire. But, in 1870 she had handed over Stalbridge to its eventual heir, her younger son, Lord Richard de Aquila Grosvenor, who, in 1886, was created Baron Stalbridge and similarly, in 1879, Fonthill to her son-in-law Sir Michael Shaw-Stewart.

In her old age she had become increasingly capricious and difficult in her relationships with her children, particularly her two sons, but she doted on

Dowager Marchioness of Westminster's memorial in Motcombe Church

Theodora and Merthyr and their only child, Elizabeth, known in the family as 'Goodie'.

She spent the winters with them at their home, Inwood House, in Henstridge and they spent the summers with her at Motcombe House. When the Duke of Westminster received a copy of the will he was dismayed and wrote angrily to Theodora saying that it had been his father's intention that all his daughters should be remembered and therefore they should receive more substantial amounts. He asked her to do what he considered simple justice and honour required by at least giving Agnes and Jane the original amount.

Theodora, having taken legal advice, did not budge. Not surprisingly therefore, at the instigation of the Duke, Lady Jane Lindsay, being most in need of financial help, was put up to oppose probate. Battle lines were drawn up, Grosvenor versus Guest, and the lawyers were about to wax fat and the press to have a field day.

The Duke's lawyers wanted to prove that Lady Westminster's mental faculties had been impaired due to her age and that her daughter had exercised undue influence over her during the preparation of the will. A private detective was employed to search for any evidence that would blacken Lady Theodora's character. He visited the Inwood area in an attempt to find out from servants and others anything that would substantiate this. Parish registers were searched to see whether she had an illegitimate child and Lady Westminster's doctor was questioned by a commission as to her mental capabilities. Eventually, his Grace, fearing the bad publicity and its effect on the good name of the family, sought a compromise which Lady Theodora's lawyers advised her to resist, and suggested that if all opposition were withdrawn, Lady Theodora would be recommended to act generously to her two sisters in the spirit of the original will. So in April 1893, the Duke, his brother and sisters did withdraw and the will and codicils were proved. However, Lady Theodora, still smarting at what she regarded as the disgraceful action of her relations, did nothing until June 1895 when she finally relented and paid Agnes and Jane a further nine thousand pounds each.

In a letter to her two sisters she expressed the hope that the unseemly brawl, which was public knowledge, would now end and more normal relations resumed. This was so in the case of Agnes but the others required more time for the wounds to heal. Slowly they did so, except for the Duke, who died in 1899 without being reconciled with his sister.

It was not until nearly thirty years had elapsed that the last of the sisters made contact with Theodora. This was, perhaps not surprisingly, Lady Jane Lindsay, who began writing pleasant letters to her estranged sister which were well received and Jane was invited to visit Inwood. This she did in October 1920 when the two sisters, now both in their eighties, were reconciled. But only just in time for nine months later Lady Lindsay died.

Lady Evelyn Grosvenor

ON the north wall of Motcombe church there is a white marble tablet in memory of Lady Evelyn Grosvenor who sadly died at the age of twelve. It may be of interest to know who she was and the cause of her early death.

Lady Evelyn was one of the large family of Richard, Earl Grosvenor and his wife, Elizabeth, later to become the second Marquess and Marchioness of Westminster.

The whole family had spent a happy Christmas together at the old Motcombe House, their Dorset residence, but early in the new year Evelyn developed typhus fever from which, due to the limited medical knowledge in those days, she did not recover and in her father's words 'the sweet child quietly resigned her innocent life on 25 January 1839'. Her funeral took place a week later when she was carried in a lead coffin to the church by six of the tenants' sons wearing white hatbands and black cloaks. She was buried inside the church but her grave appears to be unmarked.

In the following year the Grosvenors' thirteenth and last child, a girl, was born. Lord Grosvenor looked on his new daughter as a gift from God to console them for the loss of Evelyn. Therefore he expressed a wish that the baby be called Theodora which, he explained to his wife, is made up of two Greek words meaning a gift from God.

Forty-seven years later in 1887, the baby, who was now Lady Theodora Guest, gave two of the present bells to the church. One of which bears an inscription in Greek which when translated means – To the glory of God, Theodora, the gift of God, gave me [the bell].

Lord Motcombe or Lord Stalbridge?

IN 1886, the Rt. Hon. Lord Richard de Aquila Grosvenor, the younger of the two surviving sons of the second Marquess of Westminster, was awarded a peerage on the recommendation of William Gladstone in recognition of his services as Patronage Secretary to the Treasury [Chief Liberal Whip] during Gladstone's second administration between 1880-1885.

It was also through the Chief Whip that the Prime Minister had conducted most of his negotiations with Charles Parnell, the Irish national leader, which were often of a delicate and clandestine nature and sometimes involved using Mrs. O'Shea, Parnell's mistress, as an intermediary.

As a result it could be said that his peerage was well earned.

Nevertheless, like the majority of the Whig-Liberals, he was not prepared to support Gladstone's Home Rule for Ireland policy and accordingly resigned as M.P for Flintshire, which he had represented continuously since 1861.

The new peer had to decide on a title. Either Stalbridge or Motcombe seemed the most appropriate: the former because he owned the Stalbridge estate although he had no residence there: the latter because on the death of his mother, the dowager Marchioness of Westminster, he would inherit the Motcombe and Shaftesbury estates and Motcombe House would be his seat.

His wife favoured Motcombe and it is most probable that Lord Grosvenor was of the same opinion. However, sensing that his mother might not approve, he thought it right to ask her views. The eighty-eight year old dowager, now a staunch conservative, considered that the Whigs and Liberals had degenerated into 'Radicals and Revolutionists' and were being led by a maniac [Gladstone].

She left her Liberal son in no doubt as to her feelings. In her reply, she offered him no congratulations and made it plain that she would prefer that his title, as it was being given by one whose policies were, in her estimation, bringing about the ruin of the country, should not be associated with a place she loved so much as Motcombe.

Although there was no possibility of his being disinherited, as Lady Westminster had only a life interest in the estates, her son chose Stalbridge for his title, so as not to offend her, and on 22 March 1886 was created Baron Stalbridge of Stalbridge in the County of Dorset.

The Stalbridge Barony, however, was destined to last for only two generations. On the death of Lady Westminster in 1891, Lord Stalbridge took up residence at Motcombe House. In that year too he was appointed chairman of the London and North Western Railway. Two years later he decided to build a new mansion close to the old one at Motcombe which was pulled down. The cost, which was in excess of £60,000, together with the bankruptcy of some companies of which he was a director and a major creditor, meant that he had to give up living in his new home and retreat to his London residence in Bayswater where he and his wife spent the rest of their days.

The second Baron Stalbridge succeeded to the title following his father's death in 1912. After the First World War he sold the estates and Motcombe House which the first Baron had made great sacrifices to save for future generations.

The second Lord and Lady Stalbridge's marriage was not a happy one; they separated officially in 1930 but never divorced. His Lordship then devoted his time to horse breeding and sport.

A further tragedy occurred in 1930 when the twenty-five year old Stalbridge heir, an only child, was killed in a flying accident which brought about the end of the Stalbridge Barony. Since, when the second Baron died in 1949, there was no one to succeed to the title, his two brothers having pre-deceased him, leaving no male heir.

The Rt. Hon. Lord Richard de Aquila Grosvenor, First Baron Stalbridge: Politician, Railway Administrator, Channel Tunnel Proponent

Birth, Upbringing, School and University

THERE was great joy in Motcombe House, Dorset on 28th January, 1837, when the Earl and Countess Grosvenor's twelfth child was born. This time it was a much wanted boy; for, of their surviving children, eight were girls; one of the boys had died in infancy. Three years later, their thirteenth and last child was born, another girl, but sadly, in the meantime, one had died of typhus.

The infant Lord Grosvenor was christened in Motcombe Church on 2nd March when he received the name of Richard de Aquila and the local poor received an ox and about 500lbs of beef to celebrate the occasion.

The Motcombe and Shaftesbury estates then belonged to the first Marquess of Westminster, the management of which he had given to his eldest son, Earl Grosvenor, and Motcombe House on the estate had become the Grosvenors' country home where Richard spent his early childhood.

Like his brothers and sisters, he was put to a wet nurse from birth, brought up by nannies and taught by governesses. But both his parents took a keen interest in the welfare and upbringing of all their large family, and they spent as much of their time as possible at Motcombe to be in the company of their children. Earl Grosvenor, in particular, was most conscientious in his duties as a parent; he gave his children lessons with an emphasis on scripture and Bible reading, taught them games and endeavoured to instil in them the high principles by which he and his wife lived.

It would have been impressed upon them too, that duty must always come before pleasure and that wealth, however great, must never be used for extravagant and ostentatious living. Such was the atmosphere in which the young Richard grew up.

When the Marquess of Westminster died in 1845, Earl Grosvenor succeeded to the title and inherited the Grosvenor estates. He was now an extremely wealthy man; nevertheless, he still maintained his simple lifestyle.

Hugh, Richard's eldest brother, had gone to Eton but it was a decision his father had come to regret as he considered that his son and heir had acquired expensive tastes and habits while there. Therefore Richard was sent to his father's old school, Westminster, which he entered in 1849 when the headmaster was Henry George Liddell, joint author with Dr. Robert Scott of a Greek lexicon, a standard work still in use today.

Lord Richard Grosvenor when a young man

Perhaps Liddell would be better remembered as the father of the little girl, to whom his friend, Charles Dodgson (Lewis Carroll), had dedicated his two well known books, *Alice's Adventures in Wonderland* and *Through the Looking Glass.*

Although school records of Richard's progress are no longer exant, there is an excellent account of school life at that time in *Recollections of a Town Boy at Westminster* by Francis Markham, with whom Richard had formed a close friendship. There are frequent references in the book to their exploits together.

The vicinity of the Thames provided opportunities for pursuing their favourite recreations of rowing and sailing but another unauthorised and dangerous 'recreation' was playing about on the barges moored on the river. Markham relates how on one occasion his friend saved him from drowning:'

> Grosvenor and I made our way out to the furthest barge which was well out in the tideway. To get to this we had crossed a long plank. Then we were discovered by the bargee in charge, he called us to come off. Grosvenor went across the plank first and got a cuff or two from him. I then stepped on the plank, he (the bargee) took up the far end and shook it about and toppled me in the river. I could not swim. Grosvenor and the bargee ran across several planks to one that jutted out, as I swept past Grosvenor managed to catch me by one hand, held on tight and hauled me out.

Richard's involvement with the railways began in his schooldays. The author recounts that his friend often got passes for travelling on engines on the London and South Western Railway and the Great Western Railway, when they would both go to Nine Elms for a run about the goods station on a shunting engine.

A more serious pursuit occurred on wet afternoons when they were

> Always in and out the Houses of Commons together during the sessions, especially when election petitions were going on in the committee rooms.

The family suffered a grievous loss in 1854 when Richard's brother, Gilbert, died at sea while serving in the Navy, leaving Lord and Lady Westminster with only two sons.

Schooldays ended in 1855. Again following neither his brother nor his father, who had both gone to Oxford, Richard entered Trinity College, Cambridge, where he matriculated the same year. Three years later he was awarded an M.A.

Travels Abroad, Elected M.P.

AFTER University, Richard began his travels abroad. It was a time of great adventure and danger. Unfortunately, his diaries have not survived so details of dates, itineraries and travelling companions are not known. It has been established, however, that he was in the wildest region of North America living with the Sioux Indians and then the Mormons in Salt Lake City.

Finding his way across the Rockies to San Francisco, he embarked on a ship for Japan and China. In the course of his travels in that country, he visited Peking and was there in 1860 when the Emperor's Summer Palace was sacked by English and French forces.

The traveller must have returned by 1861, for in a by-election that year, he was elected Liberal M.P. for Flintshire, a constituency he was to represent for the next twenty-five years.

Flintshire was in Grosvenor territory, his father, the Marquess, owning lead mines there and other property including Halkyn Castle. Nearby were the Grosvenors' Cheshire estates with Eaton Hall their official seat.

Due probably to his high connections, Lord Richard was chosen to be chairman of an Anglo-French Committee set up in 1867, when he was aged thirty, to promote and popularise the idea of a channel rail tunnel to link England and France. This had the support of many prominent people, who saw it not only as a commercial benefit, but also the means of creating a better relationship between the two countries. Throughout his life, Lord Richard remained convinced of the great advantages that would accrue to both countries if there were a rail connection between them.

Estimates for building a tunnel at that time were put conservatively at £10m and the time for completion at nine to ten years.

Marriage, Death of First Wife and Re-Marriage

THE second Marquess died in 1869 leaving the bulk of his estates and vast fortune to his eldest son, Hugh, Earl Grosvenor, but the Dorset and Wiltshire estates were left to his widow, in her lifetime. On her death, Lord Richard would inherit the Dorset estates. In the meantime he was left £2,000 a year, which led to some correspondence in The Times by well wishers commenting on the paucity of the amount, in view of his social rank and expected life-style.

No doubt the Marquess, in all sincerity, had considered this to be a sufficient amount, bearing in mind his abhorrence of extravagant living. However, the matter was soon redressed when the Dowager Marchioness, being of a more generous nature, made over the Stalbridge portion of the Dorset estates to her youngest son. His financial position improved further in 1870 when he was elected a director of the London and North Western Railway. Two years later, his public standing was enhanced when he was made a Privy Councillor and appointed Vice-Chamberlain of Her Majesty's Household.

As a landlord of an estate of some 3,900 acres, his directorship, coupled with his recent appointments, put the thirty-seven year old bachelor in a position to seek a marriage partner within his own social class.

That person was the Hon. Beatrice Charlotte Elizabeth Vesey, youngest daughter of the third Viscount de Vesci of Abbey Leix in Ireland. The de Vescis, like the Grosvenors, who claimed Norman ancestry, were an ancient family, owning over 16,000 acres of land in Ireland.

The grand wedding took place in Westminster Abbey on 5th November 1874, before a distinguished company, including the bridegroom's brother and his wife, now the Duke and Duchess of Westminster, the Dukedom having been created earlier that year on the recommendation of William Gladstone. The Rev. Charles Kingsley, who had become a Canon of the Abbey the preceding year, was one of the three officiating clergy. He gave the blessing.

In Dorset, the occasion was marked by Lady Westminster giving a grand ball and a dinner at Shaftesbury for the tenants. Ever thoughtful for the poor, she had arranged to have 700 tickets distributed among them, enabling them to obtain provisions.

Lord Richard Grosvenor in later years

Sadly the marriage was short lived. Fourteen months later, on 15th January,1876, Lord Richard Grosvenor suffered a tragic loss; his thirty-year-old wife died at their London home, six weeks after giving birth to a daughter. She had progressed favourably after her confinement but about a fortnight before her death, she had suffered a severe attack of pleurisy, which proved fatal. It was suggested that the shock of losing her father, to whom she was closely attached, a fortnight after the baby was born, could also have been a contributory factor.

The funeral was at Eccleston, in the Grosvenor family church, near Eaton, where she was buried. In the old church at Abbey Leix, there is a fine marble memorial to this tragic lady, sculpted from a death mask, rightly described by the present Lord de Vesci as 'beautiful and haunting.'

The baby, named Elizabeth Emma Beatrice, but known in the family as Elsie, survived and was brought up in her early childhood by the de Vescis in Ireland. Here, Elsie used to be visited by her widowed father. According to family legend, it was there that he met Eleanor, youngest daughter of Robert Hamilton-Stubber of Moyne, a neighbour of the de Vescis, whom he married on 3rd April, 1879, in All Saints Church, Knightsbridge. It was a quiet wedding attended only by a few relations and close friends.

Politics and a Peerage

THE following year the Liberals won the General Election with a substantial majority. Gladstone then formed his second administration. The years 1880-1885 saw the culmination of Lord Richard's career in the House of Commons. He was appointed Government Chief Whip, also Patronage Secretary to the Treasury, thus becoming Gladstone's right-hand man and a powerful and influential figure in the Government and the Party. However, he held office at a most difficult time as the Government was beset with Irish troubles. To add to the problems, there was feuding within the party between the Radicals, led by Joseph Chamberlain, and the old Whig-Liberals. It also fell within his duties to conduct negotiations with Charles Parnell, the Irish leader; in other words to act as a go-between from Gladstone to Parnell, so that the qualities he possessed of courtesy, tact and skill as a negotiator, would certainly have been put to the test.

When in 1886 Gladstone introduced his highly contentious Home Rule for Ireland Bill, his right-hand man refused to support this move (he also had an Irish wife) and accordingly resigned.

In recognition of his services and in fulfilment of a promise by Gladstone, he was granted a Peerage, taking as his title, Baron Stalbridge of Stalbridge, a place that he owned but where he had never lived. The newly created Lord Stalbridge now joined his brother, the Duke, in the House of Lords, where he took an active part in debates when the business concerned the railways, or matters that affected them, directly or indirectly.

He first spoke in 1887 during the second reading of the Railway and Canal Traffic Bill and lastly, twenty years later, during the passage of The Cabs and Stage Carriages (London) Bill when he vigorously defended the railway companies' interests.

L.& N.W.R. locomotive Lord Stalbridge, built Crewe works 1913

Railway Chief and Lord of the Manor

Two significant events occurred during the year 1891. One was the retirement of Sir Richard Moon as Chairman of the L. & N.W.R. when Stalbridge was elected to succeed him, a post he held with distinction for the next twenty years.

The other was the death of his mother, the Marchioness, at the advanced age of ninety-four. At last, he came into his inheritance, and the estates of Motcombe, Shaftesbury and part of Gillingham, became his. Hitherto, the Stalbridge family had lived a rather nomadic life, renting various country houses during the winter, but always returning to their London home in Upper Brook Street for the summer. They now had a permanent country residence, Motcombe House, Stalbridge's boyhood home.

The Stalbridge children numbered six; sixteen-year-old Elsie, daughter of the first marriage, who had joined the family, Hugh and Blanche, twins born in 1880, Gilbert and Richard, born in 1881 and 1883, and Eleanor, born 1885.

It could not have been easy to take over from his mother, who had been associated with Motcombe and the locality for almost sixty years, during the last twenty-two of which she had 'reigned' alone. She was noted for her beneficence, liberality and concern for the welfare of 'her people'. But the new Lord of the Manor too, possessed similar qualities.

Through his genial and friendly disposition, he won over his tenants, who found him to be a sympathetic and understanding landlord. It was said that Stalbridge had a personal acquaintance with practically every inhabitant.

Despite the fact that duties in London meant that he had to spend much of his time away, he nevertheless took an active part in local affairs, particularly in his home parish of Motcombe, where he was Chairman of the Parish Council, being elected at the first Parish Meeting in 1894. He was Churchwarden at St. Mary's Church and a regular attendee at the services.

The village schools were not neglected, although the visiting was sometimes delegated to his wife and daughters. The annual treat for the schoolchildren at Motcombe House was also continued.

A New Home and Changes in the Family

IT was not long after the family had settled into their Motcombe home that it was decided to build a new mansion. The reason given was that the drains were bad, and, as a result, Stalbridge had contracted typhoid fever. Local opinion had it that the old house, by all accounts a cheerful and comfortable home, was not good enough for

The Stalbridge graves

Lady Stalbridge. The architects, Sir Ernest George and Harold Peto, were engaged to design the new mansion, which was built between 1893 and 1895. It was constructed of local red brick with dressings of Ham Hill stone in the Tudor Elizabethan style, much in vogue at that time. The new bright red bricks were in sharp contrast to the old stone building, which stood close by and was later pulled down. The cost of the new Motcombe House was said to be in the region of £60,000.

Railway Problems

IN 1902 a committee of L. & N.W.R. shareholders was formed because they were dissatisfied with the amount of the dividends, due, they claimed, to the fact that expenses were too high.

They also contended that the Company's conservative policy towards change was a contributory factor. Consequently, at the half-yearly meetings between 1903 and 1906, the Chairman and Directors were constantly harassed.

Financial Problems

IN September, 1905, Stalbridge visited the Motcombe Schools and, as was his custom, called the role. He signed the log book with the terse comment,

Called roll, all going well.

Although all was well at the school, all was certainly not well at Motcombe House. In 1887, Stalbridge, probably as an act of kindness, had entered into an agreement in support of a fellow Liberal Peer, the Lord Sudeley, who was in financial difficulties and subsequently made bankrupt. The whole affair was most complex, but Stalbridge was the principal creditor and was owed over £100,000. Recent research, instigated by the present Lord Sudeley and carried out by experts in this field, has established that the bankruptcy was quite unnecessary. There are grounds to suspect too, that this affair could have been engineered by political enemies. The consequences for the Stalbridge family were indeed grim.

First Baron and Baroness Stalbridge, with Puck

Retreat to London and Last Years

S EVERE economics had to be made. Motcombe House was abandoned and the Stalbridges, with their youngest daughter, Nellie, retreated to London to live at 22 Sussex Square, in Bayswater, where they spent the rest of their lives. The move was traumatic, particularly for Lady Stalbridge, who was now confined to an urban existence, missing greatly her country home and gardens.

For public consumption in Dorset, it was said that Lord Stalbridge had returned to London because of his many public duties there. Local gossip knew better. His action had saved Motcombe House and the estates for his son and heir, but at a great sacrifice to himself and the rest of his family.

In 1906 Nellie married Major Grant; the following year, their only child was born, a daughter called Elspeth, who became Elspeth Huxley, the author.

Stalbridge retired as Chairman of the L. & N.W.R. in February, 1911, which prompted a special article in *The Times* in tribute to his work, but he continued as a director.

Just one month later, Lady Stalbridge died and was buried in Motcombe Churchyard. On 18th May of the following year, Stalbridge died too, and made his last train journey when he was taken back to his native Motcombe to be buried with his wife.

A fine stained glass window in Motcombe Church, given by the tenantry in 1914, is one of the two memorials to him in the village. The other is the Village Hall, known as the Memorial Hall, a most attractively designed and handsome building.

Due to a variety of reasons, including the First World War, the foundation stone was first laid in 1925 but the Hall was not officially opened until 1928.

At the opening ceremony, performed by the second Lady Stalbridge, speeches were made commemorating the Lord of the Manor, who had felt keenly his duty for all those for whom he had responsibility.

His son, Hugh, who had donated the land and £200 towards the cost, did not attend. By that time he was no longer Lord of the Manor as most of the estates, which Lord Stalbridge had made such efforts to save for his son, had already been sold.

The Right Honourable Lady Theodora Guest, Grande Dame of the Old School: a Life of Good Works

NUMBER 15 Grosvenor Square on the Grosvenor Estate, which then belonged to the first Marquess of Westminster, was the London residence of his eldest son and heir, Richard third Earl Grosvenor. It was at this address that on 7 July 1840 the Earl's wife, Elizabeth, gave birth to their thirteenth and last child, a daughter. There were now eleven surviving children, eight of whom were girls. Although London born, the youngest Grosvenor spent most of her childhood and early womanhood at Motcombe House, her father's country house on the Motcombe estate, which, with the town of Shaftesbury and the Manor of Gillingham, comprised the Dorset properties owned by her grandfather, the Marquess of Westminster. On 30 August 1840 she was christened Theodora in Motcombe parish church. Her upbringing followed the usual pattern for a nobleman's daughter of that period, that is, being brought up by nursemaids and nannies and educated by governesses and tutors.

Theo was an extremely talented child who excelled in drawing, painting, embroidery and literary compositions. Whereas members of the aristocracy often continued to see as little of their offspring as possible, such was not the case with Theo's parents, who spent as much

Lady Theodora Guest

time with their children as their social and public commitments allowed.

Both parents took an active interest in their children's education. Lord Grosvenor, in particular, devoted much care and attention to their moral upbringing. He instilled in them that the privileges of high rank and great wealth carried responsibilities and duties. Lord and Lady Grosvenor themselves lived up to these principles which were later to be emulated by Theodora.

After the death of his father in 1845, Earl Grosvenor inherited the Marquisate and the ever increasing wealth derived from the Grosvenor estates in London. However affluence did not corrupt the Marquess who continued to maintain a high standard of conduct both in his public and private life. This high standard he expected of his children.

Eaton Hall, the family seat in Cheshire, now had to be occupied by the Westminsters for some part of the year and Grosvenor House for the London season. Although Theo enjoyed the social life she was always glad to return to Motcombe as she was especially fond of her Dorset home and the surrounding countryside. In a memoir dated 1864 she had written 'I love Dorsetshire so much I don't feel as if I could ever be really happy out of it.'

Lord Westminster died in 1869, leaving his widow Motcombe House and the Dorset estates for her lifetime. Also his Wiltshire properties, which included a large house, built in the Scottish baronial style at Fonthill Gifford.

Theodora now had a definite role, that of a devoted companion and support to her seventy-two year old mother who, as Lady of the Manor, had many public duties and engagements to perform, some of which her daughter undertook on her behalf. One was to lay the foundation stone of the Westminster Memorial Cottage Hospital at Shaftesbury on 25 May 1871 in memory of the late Marquess. In her speech Lady Theodora said 'I am now going, with deep gratification, to lay the foundation stone of a building which will stand for long years to come.' These were prophetic words for the building, although considerably enlarged, is still in use today as Shaftesbury Hospital.

Bittles Green, watercolour by Lady Theodora Grosvenor

Both mother and daughter took a special interest in the Motcombe schools which they visited regularly and gave the children lessons. Theodora took it upon herself to teach many of the children to read and write. She also taught in the night school which had been established in her father's time. In addition she gave talks on a variety of scientific subjects to local schools and adult audiences. With advancing years the mother left more of the schools' affairs for the attention of her daughter. Although Lady Westminster continued to finance them, it was to Lady Theodora that the headmaster went to report on school matters and to receive instructions. As well as the duties, there were the pleasurable activities; such as accompanying her mother on holidays at home and abroad, paying visits to numerous friends and relations, including Benjamin Disraeli whom they entertained in 1874 when, as prime minister, he had paid them a private visit.

Theodora, like her mother, was a staunch Conservative although the Marchioness in her younger days had been strongly Whig/Liberal as were all the Grosvenors.

Despite her many commitments, Lady Theodora found time to indulge in her favourite sport of fox hunting and did much to support the local hunts. She was reputed too to have been one of the finest horsewomen of her day.

Under the terms of her father's will she had been left £4000 a year unless she married in which case this would be reduced to £1000 a year. Again on condition that she had not married when her mother died, she had been left Pensbury House. The Dorset estates with Motcombe House would then become the property of her brother, Lord Richard Grosvenor, who was later created first Baron Stalbridge.

Pensbury was a relatively small country house dating from the middle of the eighteenth century. Although close to Shaftesbury it was, at that time, in the parish of Motcombe and within sight of Motcombe House. Attached to it was a small farm and almost 60 acres of land.

Church Farm, Motcombe, watercolour by Lady Theodora Grosvenor

Although Theodora had probably wished to have Pensbury as a home, at some time she must have changed her mind, because, in 1874, Lady Westminster purchased an estate of some 580 acres called Barcote near Faringdon, then in Berkshire now in Oxfordshire, and proceeded to build a mansion there for her daughter's eventual occupation. It was, in every respect, very much larger than Pensbury, containing many more rooms with substantial quarters for the servants and, of prime importance for its future mistress, ample stabling for her horses.

During the building of the new mansion a quite unexpected event occurred. In November 1876 thirty-six year old Theodora became engaged to thirty-eight year old Thomas Merthyr Guest, second son of the late Sir Josiah John Guest, the South Wales ironmaster. His mother, Lady Charlotte, née Bertie, was the daughter of the ninth Earl of Lindsey. Merthyr's eldest brother, Sir Ivor Guest of Canford Manor, became first Baron Wimborne in 1880.

Old Lady Westminster was overjoyed. The thought of her beloved daughter being left, in her words, 'without a protector' after her death had caused her much anxiety. She immediately wrote to Queen Victoria to acquaint her with the news. There was a long-standing friendship between the Westminsters and the Sovereign who was always kept informed of important events concerning the family.

The wedding took place on 8 March 1877 in Motcombe church. It was a time of great rejoicing.

Motcombe and Shaftesbury were crowded with visitors; the town was extensively decorated including triumphal arches bearing appropriate slogans. So too was the route from Motcombe House to the church. Many members of the Grosvenor family were present. The bride was given away by her elder brother, Hugh Lupus, now first Duke of Westminster following the creation of the dukedom in 1874.

The festivities included the roasting of an ox in the market place and a huge bonfire on Castle Hill with a firework display. Motcombe and Shaftesbury were not the only places to celebrate. Faringdon, too, marked the occasion, naturally assuming that the Guests would make Barcote their permanent home when completed.

Theodora had resolved never to leave her mother. In fact she had also resolved never to marry. In her memoir she had written, 'I can never leave my parents while they live, so I shall not marry but live with them and after, by myself, so I mean to take a little house in Dorsetshire and make an independent home.'

At least she kept one of her resolutions, she did not leave her mother, for it was agreed that the three should live together. Barcote was sufficiently completed by August 1877 to enable the Guests and Lady Westminster to move in. But in the meantime Merthyr had purchased a property at Henstridge, just over the Dorset border in Somerset. The property included Inwood, a small Georgian house, which Merthyr and Theodora proceeded to rebuild into a larger house with a tall tower, and this became their home in 1879.

They then spent the summers with the marchioness at Motcombe, with occasional stays at Barcote and Fonthill. The three would spend the winters together at Inwood.

The Guests must have preferred to make their home in the Blackmore Vale, an area which they knew so well and liked, rather than in Berkshire. Therefore it was decided to give up Barcote which was sold in 1881.

A happy event occurred in 1879 when Lady Theodora gave birth to a daughter at Motcombe House. She was christened Elizabeth Augusta Grosvenor, but was known in the family as 'Goody' and was to remain an only child.

Lady Theodora had the dual responsibility of supporting her husband on the Inwood estate and her mother on the Motcombe and Shaftesbury estates. But the latter responsibility came to an end in 1891 when the dowager marchioness died three days after her ninety-fourth birthday. A close bond had existed between mother and daughter and

Lady Theodora felt the loss very keenly. But also her connections with her old home, the village and the schools had now gone as these came into the possession of her brother, Lord Stalbridge. To make matters worse, the new Lord of the Manor decided to demolish Motcombe House and build a new mansion in its place.

Four years after the death of the Marchioness, Merthyr's mother died. Lady Charlotte has been described as one of the most outstanding and successful women of the nineteenth century. When her husband died she had taken over and run the giant Dowlais Ironworks. Also she had taken an active part in running the Guests' 11,000 acre estate at Canford. As an intellectual she is probably best remembered as the translator of the *Mabinogion* having learned Medieval Welsh to enable her to do so. Lady Charlotte was an enthusiastic collector of porcelain, the English portion of which she presented to the Victoria and Albert Museum.

Mother-in-law and daughter-in-law had got on well, for they had much in common both in their character and interests. One of the interests they shared was in collecting china and Battersea enamels, although Theodora's was on a more modest scale. Both too, were accomplished needlewomen who designed and worked some extremely fine embroidery.

Another sad year was 1904, for on 5 November Merthyr died two months before his sixty-seventh birthday. His health had been failing for some time. A cruise in the Mediterranean in their yacht with Theodora and Elizabeth and a stay at their Bournemouth home had brought no lasting improvement. He was buried at Henstridge. The hunting fraternity was much in evidence at the funeral as, like Theodora, he had a great love of hunting and had been Master of the Blackmore Vale Hunt for sixteen years.

His widow now inherited the Inwood estate which, at that time, extended over 2000 acres. The experience that she had gained when running the Motcombe estate in her mother's time was now to stand her in good stead. With the help and support of her daughter Elizabeth she built up a new life of her own. There was much to do to occupy her for her interests were wide and various. In addition to the estate there were the gardens at Inwood containing many horticultural treasures. Her Ladyship was a keen gardener and in her day employed sixteen gardeners to tend the large conservatories in which orchards and many varieties of tropical plants and fruits were grown.

Lady Theodora took a keen interest in parochial affairs. She was, for some years, a manager of the Henstridge schools, also serving on the Parish Council and the Church Council.

Her contact with Motcombe was renewed in 1906 when her brother had to give up living at Motcombe House and moved to London. She made generous financial contributions to Motcombe Church and for the coronation of George the Fifth visited the schools and gave each child a bank book and a shilling.

During the First World War, Lady Theodora did much good work in various ways in support of the war effort. One example of her practical help during those difficult years was giving shelter to some thirty Belgian refugees for a long period providing them with housing, clothes and pocket money.

Inwood House in Lady Theodora's time

The aftermath of the war brought many changes. Most of the local estates were put up for sale. In 1918 her nephew, the second Lord Stalbridge, who had inherited Motcombe and Shaftesbury after his father's death in 1912, sold Shaftesbury, also Stalbridge, another estate that he had owned which was near the Inwood estate.

The rural aristocracy was thus losing much of its power and influence, but the Grande Dame remained as a representative of the old order and a link with the society of Victorian times.

The last years of her life was marred by intractable and distressing troubles at Shaftesbury Hospital of which she was president. Speaking at one of the Hospital Committee meetings at that time, she had intimated that she had not long to live, which proved to be correct for she died on 24 March 1924 at the age of eighty-three.

It is without doubt that she had been deeply grieved by the problems at the hospital as it had been built as a memorial to her father and mother whom she greatly revered. Throughout this difficult time she had been supported by her daughter who had accompanied her to the meetings.

Lady Theodora was well known over a wide area. Throughout her long life she had taken an interest in the welfare of those amongst whom she lived considering it her duty to do so.

Many gathered at Henstridge church to pay their last respects to the kind hearted old lady of noble birth who was 'one of the old school' and who had adhered to the principle of *'noblesse oblige'*.

She was buried by the side of her husband in the enclosure set aside for the family in the churchyard.

Lady Theodora's Good Works

As one local newspaper commented 'The extent of Lady Theodora's benefactions can never be known – probably she did not know herself'.

Like her mother, her good works were done out of real kindness of heart and with a genuine desire to use her wealth for those in need. She was ever willing to lend her name and influence to any deserving cause and in later life was much in demand to open fêtes and such like functions. Those who asked her to do so would be sure of an appropriate opening speech and a generous donation to the cause. Her Ladyship's biggest single beneficent act was the building of a hospital, initially with eight beds, at Templecombe in memory of her husband, which was opened in 1906. Being close to the junction of two railway lines, it was intended primarily for railway servants and the poor who would be admitted free. Those admitted because of accidents or special emergencies who were better off would be expected to pay a small fee. All admissions, except emergencies, had to have the approval of Lady Theodora, who maintained the hospital entirely at her expense.

The following year she built and fully equipped an operating theatre at Shaftesbury hospital in memory of her mother, the cost of which was over £1000.

For the people of Henstridge she built a club room which, too, was maintained at her expense.

Her concern for the welfare of the hunt servants led her to found the Hunt Servants Benefit Society in 1872. It was liberally supported by her during her lifetime and was left £500 in her will. This registered Friendly Society is still in existence.

Her old church at Motcombe was not forgotten. To commemorate Queen Victoria's Golden Jubilee in 1887 a new ring of six bells was installed. Four of which were given by the parishioners and two, the fifth and the tenor, by Lady Theodora. They rang for the first time on Lady Westminster's ninetieth birthday on 8 November 1887.

There were innumerable causes to which Lady Theodora gave during the course of her long life. Regular beneficiaries were the Henstridge, Stalbridge and District Nursing Association, the Inwood Rifle Club, founded by Merthyr Guest, and the Blackmore Vale Football Club, which owed its inception to Lady Theodora. She always attended the annual final in Inwood grounds to present the cups and medals.

The following example is given to illustrate Lady Theodora's concern for those who were suffering real hardships. A bazaar had been held in London for the relief of the veterans of the Indian Mutiny and the Crimean War. For some reason, the Dorset survivors, numbering three, had been omitted and had received nothing. Her Ladyship, on hearing this, organised a bazaar at Inwood to provide sufficient funds so that they too could live the rest of their days with dignity rather than in squalor or in the workhouse.

Lady Theodora's Literary Works

LADY Theodora's first literary venture was in 1864 when she sent several stories she had written to the editor of a magazine called *Once a Week* who approved and published them for which she received about £12. This must have given her confidence to write more for in 1867 her first book was published called *Motcombe Past and Present*. It is, in the author's own words, 'a slight sketch of some of the points of interest in its immediate neighbourhood'. There was a second edition in 1868 and a third in 1873. The first two editions contain five plates of drawings done by the author, one of which is of Motcombe House. This little book is still much sought after by local historians and others. It is a treasured possession, handed down in some local families, particularly the presentation copies signed by the author.

By contrast her next publication was *Simple Thoughts on Bible Truths* which appeared in 1873. It is a book of fifty-two short sermons which take about five minutes to read. Each is headed with a text. There are additional ones for Christmas Day, New Year's Day and Ascension Day.

Lady Theodora was a devout Anglican but she emphasises in the preface that she has taken care to avoid all disputed and doctrinal points.

Lady Theodora Guest, Merthyr Guest, and Miss Elizabeth Guest

The book reveals that the author possessed a thorough knowledge of both the Old and the New Testaments.

The Guests travelled extensively, visiting not only Europe but also Africa, the East and America. Following a tour of the U.S.A and Canada in 1894 she published *A Round Trip in North America* in the following year. In this volume she gives many vivid descriptions of the splendid scenery on their itinerary. The author was a talented artist too and the book is enhanced by a large number of illustrations from her sketches. Having her painting materials always ready she took every opportunity to sketch not only the landscape but also the flora.

In addition to the foregoing she had printed privately a booklet explaining the meaning of botanical terms and latin words for the benefit of gardeners. In 1901 she edited *Hunting Journal of the Blackmore Vale Hounds from 1884-1888*. It consists of reports, not written by Lady Theodora, which were printed week by week in the 'Dorset County Chronicle'. But her literary output was not entirely confined to prose. She wrote and published a series of poems under the title *Summer Day Dreams* and also composed hymns for special occasions such as the flower services held at Motcombe Church.

Captain the Honourable Hugh Raufe Grosvenor 1904–1930: Sportsman and Pioneer of Aviation

I do feel that his life and death are an inspiration because he stood for all that is best in our generation and there were few like him – one would really give anything to have some of his courage, daring and modesty.
Elspeth Huxley.

O N the 18 August 1904 the Mayor and Corporation of Shaftesbury received a telegram from Lord Stalbridge, landlord of the Motcombe, Shaftesbury and Stalbridge estates, announcing that on the previous night a grandson and heir to the title and his estates had been born, also that both the mother and baby were progressing well.

A message of congratulations was immediately sent on behalf of the Corporation and Burgesses to the parents, the Honourable Mr. and Mrs. Hugh Grosvenor at their London address in Eaton Place, and the bells of St. Peter's church were rung during the day in honour of the event.

It was reported, too, that much delight was expressed in the adjoining village of Motcombe when the news was made known, for Lord Stalbridge, whose seat was at Motcombe House, was considered a good landlord who was held in high esteem by his tenants.

All now seemed set fair for the Stalbridge line to continue for many years to come.

Two months later the infant was brought to Motcombe church where, before a large congregation, which included the village school children, he was christened Hugh Raufe by the Reverend Neville Lovett, Vicar of Shanklin, Isle of Wight, a cousin of the boy's mother.

A local newspaper, in reporting this event, expressed the hope that the

Captain the Hon. Hugh Raufe Grosvenor, 'Puck'

newly born heir would, in the far distant future, succeed to the title and estates fulfilling his duties with the same grace and courtesy as his grandfather.

As a member of the ancient house of Grosvenor, Hugh Raufe had an impeccable pedigree: the Grosvenors claimed Norman ancestry from Gilbert Le Gros Veneur who was a nephew of Hugh Lupus, Earl of Chester, nephew of William the Conqueror.

Lord Stalbridge, who was formerly Lord Richard de Aquila Grosvenor, had been raised to the peerage in recognition of his services as Liberal Chief Whip during Gladstone's second ministry from 1880-1885. He was the youngest son of Richard, second Marquess of Westminster and brother of Hugh Lupus, named after his Norman ancestor, who had been created first Duke of Westminster in 1874.

Whereas his father's family were of the nobility, his mother's were gentry. Her maiden name was Gladys Elizabeth Nixon, younger daughter of Brinsley De Courcy Nixon. The Nixons were of Scottish descent but had gone over to Ireland at the time of the Ulster Plantation in the reign of James I. They had become established in Fermanagh and Cavan but Brinsley's branch of the family must have returned at some time to their native Scotland for he had been born in Edinburgh.

He was a successful businessman and a banker, a founder member of the London and Provincial Bank, also chairman and director of several companies, some of which operated in Russia.

His daughter Gladys was described as petite, charming and very beautiful. According to family legend, Hugh Grosvenor had met her, fallen in love, proposed and had been accepted all within the space of four days.

Although the Stalbridge heir's first name was Hugh, he was generally called Raufe, but within the family and amongst friends he was known as 'Puck' and continued to be so for the rest of his life. The originator of this was his mother who had likened his childish pranks, practical jokes and happy-go-lucky attitude to Shakespeare's character of that name.

Puck's early childhood was spent at Child Okeford Manor, near Blandford, his parents' country home. He was an only child but, before going to a private school, had for companionship four girl cousins, Margaret, Joan and Constance, daughters of Captain, later Colonel, James and the Honourable Blanche Holford, his father's twin sister and Elspeth, daughter of Josceline and Eleanor Grant, his father's youngest sister.

Elspeth, who was staying with the Holfords while her parents were in Kenya, was later to become well-known in the literary world as Elspeth Huxley the author.

Of these four cousins, Margaret 'Peggy' was Puck's favourite. They became close friends and remained so until his untimely end.

Holidays were often spent at the Nixons' country home at Westward Ho!, Devon. Here Puck became acquainted with his cousins on his mother's side. Her two brothers, Fergus and Brinsley, and her sister Charlotte all had children.

With the death of Lord Stalbridge in May 1912, the Honourable Hugh Grosvenor accordingly inherited the title and the estates. Due to acute financial problems, the first Baron had been compelled to give up living at Motcombe House for the last few years of his life and had lived in London. He had been determined to leave his estates to his eldest son intact at all costs, so sacrifices had had to be made, the brunt of which had fallen on his wife and other children, thus giving rise to much resentment.

The new Lady Stalbridge had been very fond of her father-in-law and felt that her son possessed many of his qualities. She wrote:

> He had a most charming personality. There was about him a great simplicity and merriment of heart, his presence radiated kindness and goodness he was beloved by all who knew him. Those who came to live at Motcombe found themselves surrounded by an atmosphere of affection and esteem. In Puck's character there were many qualities reminiscent of his grandfather – the same kindliness of heart and friendliness of spirit. Each seemed to possess some inward quality that endeared them to their fellow men.

Puck's parents first took up residence at Motcombe House in January 1914. Their home was a modern brick-built mansion that had been completed in 1895, replacing the old Motcombe House which had stood nearby. The new building was described by a relative as 'a great barrack of a place with no sense of comfort.'

On the evening of their arrival, a band of villagers proceeded to the mansion to meet their new squire, his wife and his son. An address of welcome was read in which the heir, then in his tenth year, was included with the hope that he would also prove a worthy scion of the noble House of Grosvenor.

His Lordship's stay however was short due to the outbreak of the First World War the following August, when he rejoined the army and was away for the duration, returning from time to time when on leave.

The war also affected Puck's schooling; he had to return home from his school at Westgate and continue his education with a governess but was able to go back again before starting at Eton, his father's *Alma*

Mater, in the summer term of 1918 just before his fourteenth birthday.

In September of that year, an event took place which was to have a considerable effect on the heir's inheritance. Lord Stalbridge decided to sell a substantial part of his estates, some 8150 acres including the towns of Shaftesbury and Stalbridge and what was termed the outlying portions of the Motcombe Estate, which included farms and cottages in Marnhull, Todber, Stour Provost, East Stour and West Orchard. But the main part of the Motcombe Estate including Motcombe House was retained, at least for the time being.

Raufe Grosvenor enjoyed his time at Eton where he acquired a new name 'Grubby' not because of any aversion to soap and water but because of the wonderful hampers of food sent from Motcombe by his mother, which he and his friends were able to enjoy.

A strong bond existed between mother and son. They had much in common and corresponded daily, the son receiving a chronicle of events at Motcombe and the mother a summary of the happenings at Eton, mostly concerning sporting activities.

Although keen on all sports at school, it was at boxing that he excelled. His pugilistic career had begun at Motcombe, where, shortly after her arrival, Lady Stalbridge had started a scout troop. The squire's son had been encouraged by his mother to mix with boys of his own age in the village so he had joined the troop. They were taught to box by the Vicar and one of the farmers, a heavyweight of repute. At Eton, Raufe boxed

Hugh, 2nd Baron Stalbridge, and son, the Hon. Hugh Raufe Grosvenor

for the school in various school and inter-school competitions losing only one contest during his time there.

Like his mother, he was of small build thus he began as a Paperweight at seven stone six pounds, progressing through Fly and Bantam weight to finish as a Featherweight at nine stone.

School reports indicated that he did well in the subjects which appealed to him, English Literature and History being his best. Comments too were made on his character:

> He is altogether a delightful boy to have to deal with, very high spirited but very amenable. He has the faults of his virtues, he is bright, quick and often careless in consequence and too impetuous in his work.

After Eton came Christ Church, Oxford, which he entered in 1923 to read for a degree in Rural Economy.

It was when at University that he began his career as a steeplechase jockey. As the son of a country squire, he had naturally learnt to ride at an early age. His father had been Master of the South West Wilts Hunt so horses and hounds had played a large part in his early life. The son had inherited from his father the love of horses and equestrian sport. Both had great skill in horsemanship.

Lord Stalbridge was the owner and trainer of racehorses. It was on his horse 'The Saint IV' that Raufe won his first steeplechase at Cardiff in 1925. Among other notable successes were winning the Cheltenham Gold cup on Lord Stalbridge's 'Thrown In' in 1926 and the Valentine Steeplechase at Liverpool in the same year. He also rode 'Thrown In' in the Grand National in 1926 and 1927. In the first year he finished eighth but in the second, had the misfortune to be thrown at the first fence suffering what was called 'Real National Luck'. His equestrian skills however were not confined to steeple chasing. He excelled too in polo playing. It was while playing this game that he took to wearing high-necked jumpers. Others were to follow, thus starting the fashion of wearing what became known as polo-neck sweaters for everyday wear.

His versatility as a sportsman was demonstrated by his skill as a yachtsman. He was one of the crew of his father's yacht 'Tally Ho' when it won the Ocean Yacht Race in a north westerly gale in 1927, being one of the only two yachts to complete the race.

The Honourable Hugh Raufe Grosvenor came of age in August 1925 when there were two days of celebrations at Motcombe. On the first day the schoolchildren were entertained by Lord and Lady Stalbridge in the grounds of Motcombe House. On the following day it was the turn of the tenants, farmers and villagers. The young squire, who was very popular in the village, was presented with a list containing the names of some 500 tenants, villagers and schoolchildren who had subscribed towards a gift to mark the occasion. Raufe Grosvenor thanked everyone for their kindness and generosity, saying that he intended to use the money they had donated to give a billiard table to the Memorial Hall which was to be built in the village in memory of his grandfather.

The event, however, was tinged with sadness and irony for Lord Stalbridge had already contracted to sell the Motcombe estate including Motcombe House and was in the process of negotiating to buy a property, Warsash House, near Southampton not far from Hamble where his yacht and other boats were moored.

His Lordship, in his speech, took the opportunity of explaining, rather apologetically, why he was selling up and leaving. This, he said, was due to heavy taxation and death duties and there was no other option.

In the previous month he had made a speech at the South West Wilts Puppy Show pointing out that his action had been motivated in the best interests of his son and heir.

But it was said that his son, Lady Stalbridge and other members of the family were unhappy with his decision and had tried to dissuade him from doing so. Also the two trustees of the estate, friends of the first Lord Stalbridge had demonstrated their disagreement by resigning.

Lord Stalbridge's plan was to use the money raised by the sale to provide the capital for a private limited company, 'The H.R. Company', in which he and his son would be the principle shareholders.

By way of compromise, he had not sold Stalbridge Park Farm with about 700 acres of land. His intention was to build a house there which would be the Stalbridge seat and would eventually be occupied by his heir when he succeeded to the title.

A year later, the Honourable Hugh Raufe Grosvenor left Oxford with a B.A. in Rural Economy and began his short career in the 7th Hussars. Army life in peacetime was not to his liking. He found it too boring so he resigned, leaving with the rank of Captain but remaining on the supplementary reserve.

The final phase of his short life began in April 1928 when he was appointed Aide-de-Camp to the

The Hon. Hugh Grosvenor's memorial in Australia

Governor of South Australia, Sir Alexander Hore-Ruthven V.C., later to become the Earl of Gowrie and Governor-General of Australia.

His reasons for doing so are not known, but it is suggested that his self-indulgent lifestyle, although he derived much enjoyment from his sporting activities, was not really satisfying and he sought to be of some service to his Country and the Empire. The Grosvenors, in general were noted for their sense of public duty.

At first it was thought that he would find the duties too tedious with the constant round of official functions and having to be agreeable at all times to all manner of people but, sometime after, the Governor indicated in a letter to Lady Stalbridge that he was well pleased with his aide.

Even if his duties were tedious at times, Australia offered opportunities in other directions, especially in flying which had become the ADC's great passion.

He had first learnt to fly at the Hampshire Aerodrome Club at Hamble near the Stalbridge's home at Warsash and had made his first solo flight in February 1927. Five months later he gained his Royal Aeronautical Society Certificate. Not long after his arrival in Australia, he had acquired a Moth aeroplane and his happiness was complete.

His first aerial adventure happened during the course of his official duties when flying the Governor to open a fête. A gale was blowing and, although the landing was safely accomplished, the machine then turned upside down leaving His Excellency and his aide in that position. Fortunately neither was hurt, only somewhat shaken. After a stiff drink, the Governor proceeded to open the fete and the aide, who had a great sense of humour, composed a humorous poem entitled *A Ballad of the Air on the Tribulations of His Excellency*.

Captain Grosvenor's next aerial adventure was an epic flight of 8000 miles round Australia in his Moth in May 1929 which he accomplished solo in sixteen flying days averaging about 500 miles a day, during the course of which, when at Darwin, he abandoned his own flight for a time in order to look for two English airmen who had been reported missing during their flight from England. He flew many hundreds of miles over land and sea in a vain effort to find them, but later news came that they had been found alive and well. Exactly four weeks after setting out he arrived in Adelaide, having completed his record flight without mishap.

This made a great impression in Australia and received wide publicity in the press. He was praised and admired for his courage and skill. Many letters of congratulations were received from Governors of States and schoolboys alike. One letter in particular sums up the feeling when the writer asks permission 'to add my humble tribute of admiration to the universal chorus which salutes your great adventure of flying round Australia. It was a great feat of courage, confidence, skill and knowledge. Alone you did it without fuss or advertisement.'

But the intrepid aviator was not content to rest on his laurels. In the summer of that year, plans were being made for a flight between Australia and England to attempt to beat the existing record which had been established by Squadron Leader Kingsford-Smith who had just completed the journey of 10,500 miles in 12 days 21½ hours.

A cable was sent to his cousin, The Duke of Westminster*, asking whether he would finance the proposed flight in the interests of aviation. This he consented to do.

The aeroplane, a Lockheed Vega monoplane, was to be called 'Bend'Or' the name the Duke was known by.

But all this was not to be for, on 6 January 1930, a terrible tragedy occurred and the young nobleman's life was ended.

The last flight he made before the fatal accident was only a few days before, at Christmas time. It was in response to an urgent message from Kangaroo Island, about 70 miles from Adelaide, stating that a twelve-year-old schoolboy was seriously ill and needed to be brought to the Adelaide Hospital, there being no resident doctor on the island and no pilot available. The boy was a scout and so was Captain Grosvenor who volunteered at once to go, considering it his duty to do so, although the weather was atrocious. He flew to the island in a terrible rainstorm, landing in a sea of mud, and returned safely with the sick boy three hours later. But despite his heroic effort the boy died several days later.

This attempt to save a life was his last public act and his farewell good deed. As someone wrote 'It was typical of him that his last flight should have been made in the service of suffering humanity.'

It was an act which endeared him to the people of South Australia.

The day before the disaster took place; Captain Grosvenor had gone to Melbourne and had called at the Australian Branch of the Shell Company, Point Cook, to discuss final details of the proposed flight to England in March. He had made arrangements to take Flight Lieutenant F.A.Briggs of the Royal Australian Air Force with him as co-pilot. The two of them, accompanied by Leading Aircraftsman D.C.Ewen, then went out for a short trial flight in a Wackett Widgeon II flying boat and were returning to the aerodrome when, at a height of about 400 feet, the machine suddenly nose-dived, striking the water about a mile from the shore and sank.

* The second Duke, Hugh Richard Arthur, (1879-1953). He was, in fact, a second cousin.

Although an extensive search was made, the bodies were never found and it was assumed that they had been washed away. The wreck of the aircraft was found and brought to the surface. Various theories were advanced as to the cause of the crash but nothing conclusive was ever established.

The tragic news had to be cabled to Lord and Lady Stalbridge who were naturally devastated by the loss of their only son and heir of whom they had such high hopes. Their marriage had not been a happy one so they had separated but were reunited for a time following the tragedy.

But it was a triple tragedy. Flight Lieutenant Briggs's wife and five-year-old daughter had just set sail for England, expecting to meet her husband after his arrival, when the news was broken. Leading Aircraftsman Ewen's wife lost her husband after a marriage of only fourteen days.

The accident was widely reported in the press both here and in Australia. There were countless messages of sympathy, including many from the people of South Australia, by whom he was regarded as a hero. On the following Sunday, the 12 January, a memorial service was held in Motcombe Church attended by Lord and Lady Stalbridge, other members of the family, and a large congregation who had come to pay their last respects to one who had been well known and greatly liked in the village. The service was conducted by the Vicar, the Reverend E.C. King, who had been his boxing instructor when in the scouts.

Three days later, another service was held in the Grosvenor Chapel, South Audley Street, London, at which other relatives, including the Duchess of Westminster and members of the nobility were present. The Bishop of Portsmouth officiated. He had, when Vicar of Shanklin, performed the christening ceremony at Motcombe in 1904.

In Adelaide, a memorial service for the three airmen took place in St. Peter's Cathedral on the 2 February. The sermon was preached by the Bishop of Adelaide who referred to Hugh Grosvenor as an adventurous spirit and a pioneer of aviation who had sought no prize, but the prize had come in the love and admiration he had gained from his fellows.

At the suggestion of a local newspaper, a fund was started to provide a memorial to the late airman in the form of a cot in the Adelaide Children's Hospital. It was felt that this would be a fitting memorial, as Captain Grosvenor was a hero to children and a lover of children, and who, as a scout leader, was nearly always surrounded by groups of youngsters asking questions about aeroplanes which he had patiently tried to answer.

The newspaper published daily details of subscriptions received, some of which were from children, until the required amount was reached. Then, at a simple ceremony, the cot was dedicated in memory of 'a very gallant gentleman'.

A more conventional memorial was erected about three hundred miles from Adelaide on what was known as the Grosvenor Landing Ground which was, in fact, a small aerodrome. Captain Grosvenor was the first pilot to have landed there. It was unveiled by the Governor on 1 May 1930.

A third memorial in the village church at Motcombe is in the form of a bronze angel with the inscription 'He leaves a white unbroken glory, a gathered radiance, a width, a shining peace, under the night.

> To the memory of the Honourable Hugh Raufe Grosvenor only son of the 2nd Baron Stalbridge. Killed flying in Australia January 6th 1930 aged 25 years.

It is situated next to the stained glass window in memory of his grandfather, the first Baron Stalbridge, whom he had so much resembled in character and ways.

Memorial to Hon Hugh Raufe Grosvenor in Motcombe Church

Lady Stalbridge never recovered from the loss of her son. When the wreck of the aircraft was brought to the surface, the remains of his wristwatch were found strapped to the fuselage. It was sent home to her and served as a message of farewell and an inseparable link with Puck, for, although only the frame remained, she always wore it, day and night, in his memory.

There was no third Baron Stalbridge. The heir to the title, Lord Stalbridge's youngest brother, The Honourable Gilbert Grosvenor, had died in 1939 without a male heir. Therefore when Hugh Stalbridge himself died on Christmas Day 1949 the title became extinct.

Some time before his death Lady Stalbridge had returned to live with her husband at Pounds Farm, near Newbury. But they did not remain united in death. Lord Stalbridge was buried in the family grave at Motcombe. His widow however was, at her express wish, cremated at Brookwood.

Gladys Elizabeth, Baroness Stalbridge

For kind hearts are more than coronets. And simple faith than Norman blood.
Tennyson

WHEN it was announced that the Hon. Hugh Grosvenor, an officer in the fourteenth Hussars and eldest son of Richard de Aquila Grosvenor, first Baron Stalbridge, was going to marry Miss Gladys Elizabeth Nixon, some of his relatives did not approve.

It had been assumed that the heir to the Stalbridge barony as a member of the ancient House of Grosvenor, who claimed Norman ancestry, would choose a partner from within the ranks of the aristocracy or the landed gentry, but his future wife was from neither. The Nixons at that time would probably have been considered gentry. They did not have landed estates although at one time some branches of the family had owned estates in Ireland. To make matters worse in the eyes of Hugh's class-conscious relatives, Gladys' father, Brinsley de Courcy

Lady Stalbridge

Nixon was in trade. He was chairman and director of several companies and a director of the London and Provincial Bank.

The feelings of Hugh's parents towards his choice of bride are not known but those of his aunt, Lady Theodora Guest, a Grosvenor by birth, are. She considered that her nephew had disgraced the whole family and that 'Nixey' was not a lady. In later years however, Lady Theodora's opinion changed and she was very supportive of her nephew's' wife.

The wedding took place at St. Jude's Church, South Kensington on 10 November 1903 and the honeymoon was spent at Motcombe House, Dorset, Lord Stalbridge's seat, which would one day be theirs.

In the following year a son and heir was born at their London home. He was christened Hugh Raufe, but became known in the family as 'Puck'. There were no other children and his tragic death in a flying accident in 1930 led to the extinction of the Stalbridge barony.

In addition to their London home in South Audley Street, the Grosvenors had a country house, Child Okeford Manor, about ten miles from Motcombe, which continued to be their Dorset home until January 1914, when they took up residence at Motcombe House as Lord and Lady Stalbridge, Hugh having succeeded to the title on the death of his father in 1912.

Seven months later, following the outbreak of the First World War, Lord Stalbridge rejoined the army leaving his wife to cope alone. This she did exceedingly well having already adapted to her role as lady of the manor. She had lost no time in forming a Boy Scout troop with a bugle band in Motcombe and for several years she was president

She became very active too in the local nursing association. It was in this area that she again encountered Lady Theodora Guest who was noted for her good works and found 'Nixey's' sense of duty much to her liking; for although her niece was not of noble birth she was certainly noble in character. This quality, as would later emerge, was lacking in her husband.

During the traumatic war years Lady Stalbridge played a leading part in organisations in support of the war effort, although in private she decried the war and the stupidity of those responsible.

The Red Cross and Queen Mary's Needlework Guild, which provided comforts for the troops at the front, occupied much of her time. Concerts were held at Motcombe House in support of these concerns. On one occasion at least, the concert took the form of a fantasia with music written by Lady Stalbridge in which members of her family including her son, as well as some of the Motcombe scouts, took part. Wounded soldiers from Gillingham formed part of the audience.

Her many good deeds in Motcombe during the war and after earned her the love and respect of all. There were many instances of personal kindness and generosity both to individuals in the village and to members of her own family; both Grosvenors and Nixons, which led a prominent parishioner to refer to her as 'a Florence Nightingale to the people of Motcombe, who had clothed the poor, fed the hungry and ministered to the sick'. One grateful relative described her as 'the sweetest, kindest friend I ever had, always understanding and forgiving'.

Despite all this she was still not quite accepted by her husband's relatives ever conscious of their lineage.

The year 1918 brought peace again, but not at Motcombe House following the return of his Lordship. Their marriage had not proved to be a success perhaps because they had so little in common. Gladys, intelligent, artistic and sophisticated did not share Hugh's love of country pursuits, particularly blood sports, which she found abhorrent. Once she released a fox which her Master of Fox Hounds husband had shut up ready to be released for hunting thus incurring his fury. However she did share his interest in racing possibly due to their son having made a name for himself as a jockey.

In 1925, there was further trouble when Lord Stalbridge decided to sell his Motcombe estate. He had already disposed of the Shaftesbury and Stalbridge estates in 1918, thus obtaining a very substantial amount of money which should have enabled him to retain Motcombe. His wife considered it to be his duty to do so as his father had made considerable sacrifices to enable his son to inherit the estates unencumbered. Hugh, however, had not inherited the Grosvenor's sense of duty – the principle of *noblesse oblige* – so Motcombe was sold and the Stalbridges moved to Warsash but lived separate lives although they never divorced.

Lady Stalbridge's links with Motcombe were not entirely severed; she did return to open some of the annual flower shows when she was always sure of a warm welcome. Ever conscious of her duty, she made a point of visiting those who were unable to see her at these events.

The Stalbridges were re-united for a time when Lady Stalbridge went to nurse her sick husband at his farm near Newbury where he died on Christmas Day 1949.

His widow left Warsash and spent her remaining years at Hove. She was not buried with her husband at Motcombe following her death in 1960 but, in accordance with her wishes, was cremated at Brookwood.

Margaret Green née Holford

THERE can now be no-one alive today in Motcombe and around who will remember Margaret 'Peggy' Holford who died on 18 July 1996 at her home near Ipswich aged 94.

She was born at Motcombe House and christened in Motcombe church in 1902, the eldest of the three daughters of Colonel and the Hon. Mrs. Holford. Her mother, Blanche, was the twin sister of Hugh, the second Lord Stalbridge. She spent most of her childhood at Cherry Orchard Farm and Motcombe House. Peggy and her cousin Raufe Grosvenor 'Puck', the Stalbridge heir, were great childhood friends. He was killed in a flying accident in 1930.

Her marriage to John Everard Green at Motcombe Church in 1923 was a notable event when some of the village children scattered flowers in the path of the bride and groom and Lord Stalbridge, 'Uncle Hughie', sounded a hunting horn.

Although her connections with Motcombe had long ceased, she still had vivid memories of her childhood here and had some amusing anecdotes to tell of people and events in Motcombe long ago.

She was remembered as a kind and courteous old lady, definitely one of the old school who retained and lived up to the standards and values of her generation.

Just nine days after her death, her elder son, Sir Richard Green, died of cancer at the age of 61. He was a former chairman of Lloyds Insurance.

Margaret Green was a cousin of Elspeth Huxley, the author, who also has Motcombe connections through her mother, formerly the Hon. Eleanor Grosvenor, Lord Stalbridge's youngest sister.

She was known in the family as 'Nellie' and from the age of seven lived at the old Motcombe House and then in the new one after it's completion in 1895.

The Late Mrs Elspeth Huxley

ELSPETH Huxley the author, who died in January 1997, aged 89, had connections with Motcombe through her mother, the Hon. Mrs. Eleanor Grant, youngest sister of the second Baron Stalbridge; although Elspeth herself used to spend her school holidays during the First World War with her aunt the Hon. Blanche Holford, at Cherry Orchard

Farm near Shaftesbury and visited Motcombe House when her 'Uncle Hughie' was home on leave.

There is much about Motcombe in her book *Nellie Letters from Africa*. Although there are several inaccuracies, which she acknowledged, it makes interesting reading.

She once paid a visit to Port Regis School, formerly Motcombe House, her mother's childhood home, which had been built by her grandfather, the first Baron Stalbridge.

Many changes have taken place there since those times but Elspeth considered that its present role as a school would have met with his approval.

2
Motcombe People

Triumph and Tragedy: the Story of a Motcombe Family

IN 1847 Albinus Reeves, a widower, George and Martha Reeves, his son and daughter-in-law and their five children, Mary, James, Jabez, Jonathan and Jeremiah, were evicted from their home at Motcombe on the orders of Samuel Ullett, land agent for the Marquess of Westminster, due to rent arrears extending over two years. The account books of the Marquess's lawyers record that on 5 October 1846 they had written to George Reeves for payment of the arrears and that three days later they had paid a visit to Albinus and had, in their words, 'endeavoured to bring him to some terms of arrangement as to the two years of rent due but without effect as he completely set us at defiance.' This led to a distraint order being served on Albinus and George. Shortly after a further effort was made, according to the lawyers, 'to bring the matter to an amicable arrangement, but, after a long conference, Reeves declined to come to any understanding and determined to let the matter take its course.' Having failed in their endeavours, they sent an appraiser and a cart and items were removed from the home. A final effort was made, this time to try and agree the terms on which the recalcitrant tenant would be prepared to give up possession of the house and garden but 'he at length declined to agreeing to any terms short of being allowed a life interest in the property.'.

So the Reeves' family now had to face eviction which did not take place until June the following year, thus allowing them time to make plans for their future. For Albinus however, now sixty-one years old, there was to be no new beginning. What lay ahead was dire poverty leading to the workhouse and petty crime resulting in five terms of imprisonment, albeit of short duration, in Dorchester jail, where he died.

The ill-fated Albinus Reeves was born at Gillingham in 1785, the sixth and last surviving child of Edward Reeves, a shoemaker, and his wife, Elizabeth née Down. His grandfather, also named Edward, had been appointed parish clerk of Gillingham in 1748. Of the several parish offices, that of parish clerk was the most prestigious and the appointment was usually for life. Gillingham was a 'peculiar' meaning that it was exempt from the jurisdiction of the bishop; it also had the power of probate of wills. Therefore the parish clerk held a responsible position which would have enhanced his status in the parish. Obviously he was literate and so too was his shoemaker son, but this ability did not extend to at least two of the latter's children, Albinus and Edward, nor were they apprenticed to a trade. This is evident when the two brothers were co-makers of a bond on the occasion of Albinus' marriage to Lydia Burt in 1806. Both made their mark instead of signing their names and gave their occupations as labourers. Nevertheless Albinus had married well, for his bride was a daughter of Thomas Burt, described as a yeoman and gentleman of Thorngrove Farm, Gillingham. He was the tenant of a large farm and also owned property in the area. The term 'gentleman' was usually applied to those in the professions but for persons such as Thomas Burt it signified that he was of considerable standing in the local community, much superior to the tradesmen and shopkeepers and, as in his case, a trustee of one or more of the parochial charities. His wife was a daughter of William and Frances Broadway of Motcombe. William was a wealthy yeoman and the owner of a fair amount of land. His wife had inherited a substantial fortune thus elevating their position and bringing them into the ranks of the lesser gentry. Their imposing table tomb in Motcombe churchyard is evidence of the social status they had enjoyed. With such connections Albinus' prospects seemed promising.

About two years after their marriage Albinus and Lydia with their first-born, Eliza, moved to Motcombe where Thomas Burt owned a small farm. It appears that initially Albinus worked for his father-in-law and then became the tenant of his farm because at the baptism of their sixth and last child in 1814, he describes himself as a farmer.

When Thomas Burt died in 1820 Lydia received her share of his estate including three and a half acres of land at Motcombe which Albinus mortgaged; a part to Benjamin Baverstock, a Primitive Methodist, whose wife was a cousin of Lydia and the remainder to William Jenkins, possibly another relation. With the inheritance they may have built a new home at Motcombe. Unfortunately their inheritance had come at the wrong time: the end of the Napoleonic Wars had resulted in a severe agricultural depression causing great hardship to the farmers and even greater for the labourers leading to the riots of the 1830s. The parish records reveal that times were very bad for the Reeves. Albinus, who had once paid the poor rate, had now come to the parish for work and was in receipt of poor relief.

In 1836 Albert George, the fourth of Albinus and Lydia's children, married Martha Arnold a neighbour's daughter. Albert George was known by his second name and in the 1841 census, he, with his wife and a family of three, are shown living with his parents. The location of their home at Motcombe is indicated on the tithe map of about that time. It gives the owner and occupier as Albinus Reeves and the area of land fifteen perches. The death of Lydia Reeves in December 1842 and of Benjamin Baverstock a year or so earlier marked a further decline in this family's fortunes. It appears that Baverstock, because of family connections, may have supported the Reeves financially and had had an interest in their home. If this had been the case it all came to an end when his widow sold her property to the Marquess of Westminster which culminated in the Reeves losing their home. The true circumstances may never be known but Albinus was convinced that he had a lifetime entitlement to the property and, according to family legend, 'they were deprived of their holdings in that locality by the scheming of wealthy landlords'. Too much reliance on verbal understandings and Albinus' illiteracy may well have played a part.

The eviction saw the parting of the ways between Albinus and the rest of his family. He returned to his native Gillingham and in the 1851 census is recorded as living with relations. Two years earlier he had been caught stealing iron from a gate and was sentenced to fourteen days imprisonment with hard labour. His downward path continued; his next abode was Shaftesbury Union Workhouse. It is not known when he had entered this institution but in 1861 he again received a jail sentence of fourteen days for causing a disturbance there. This was his fourth conviction. Details of his other two convictions have not come to light but they are most likely to have been of a petty nature.

His fifth and final spell in prison came a few months later, in April 1861, when he received a sentence of fourteen days with hard labour for stealing potatoes.

His death occurred a few days later at the age of seventy-five. He died suddenly and alone in his cell after finishing his work at the hand-mill. There was a coroner's inquest and the jury unanimously decided that he had died by the 'Visitation of God' and was accordingly buried in the prison cemetery. So ended the tragic life of Albinus Reeves.

Fortunately George Reeves and family were eventually to fare better. After their eviction they moved to Ebbw Vale where George was employed as a coal coker in the ironworks. The question arises why they went to South Wales. The answer may be with the Primitive Methodist chapel at Motcombe which George and Martha attended and where some of their children were baptised.

Benjamin and Frances Baverstock were also members, so too was Robert Tuffin, a cousin of Martha's and a contemporary. He became a minister and in 1847 was appointed to the Tredegar circuit which included Ebbw Vale. The plight of the Reeves family would have been common knowledge among the chapel attendees at Motcombe. It is likely that help was sought for them and Martha's kinsman may well have come to their aid by securing a home for the family and a job for George at Ebbw Vale. It was a big adjustment to make from a cottage in rural surroundings to a terraced house in an industrial area and the dirt and grime of the ironworks. But the Reeves were not alone, large numbers were deserting the land to find work and a better life with opportunities in the expanding industrial regions.

It was George and Martha's sons who were to benefit most from the move. After receiving a basic schooling they joined the local workforce and acquired skills in various aspects of the iron and steel works. Such skills were highly marketable and provided them with the opportunity to travel and eventually to prosper. This is what Jabez, the second son, did in 1865 when he emigrated to the United States where, according to the family, he had a job waiting for him at Niles, Ohio. He had arrived at the right place and at the right time. The Civil War had just ended and war damage repair, together with the expansion of the railways, had created a huge demand for steel. His brothers Jonathan and Jeremiah followed him in 1867. Finally three years later the fourth brother, Albert George, joined his brothers. He had been born after the family had arrived in Wales.

The boom continued, so in 1872, the brothers took the plunge and branched out on their own. They established the Reeves Brothers Boiler Works in Niles where steam boilers, oil tanks and blast furnace stacks were manufactured. The employees originally numbered about thirty-four in the plant and twice as many on site setting up items. One brother, Jonathan, for reasons unknown, sold his interest in the business and returned to Wales where he married. He never returned to Ohio.

The others continued to prosper and expanded into other business ventures. Jeremiah founded the Reeves Banking and Trust Company in Dover, Ohio. Jabez became involved in a land development company and Albert George held directorships in several banks and owned business property. At the beginning of the last century the Reeves business empire had over a thousand employees and was one of the largest employers in the area. They were much involved in other ways, particularly in the social and economic betterment of their communities. Albert George, for example, endowed a Chair of History at a local college. When Jeremiah died in 1920 his estate was valued at about a million and a half dollars. By dint of hard work, industry, perseverance and determination they had triumphed and had been rewarded.

During the course of the last century much has changed in the iron and steel industry. The areas where the Reeves had their businesses contain many closed steel works and only one with a Reeves connection remains today. That is the Greer Steel Company in Dover, Ohio, operated by a great-grandson of Jeremiah.

What became of the parents of the successful brothers? Their father followed them to the U.S.A where he was employed in a supervisory capacity in one of his son's steelworks. It is doubtful whether Martha ever went. If she had, she must have returned, as she died at Abergavenny in 1887. Of the other siblings, Mary, the eldest, who had been widowed in 1868, emigrated with her family to Ohio in the same year as her mother's death. She was ten when the family left Motcombe and probably had vivid memories of the hardships they had endured. The remaining brother, James, stayed in Wales until his premature death in 1875 at the age of thirty-six.

One wonders whether the family kept in touch with Albinus and knew of the appalling circumstances surrounding his last years, we shall in all probability never know but the story of their contrasting fortunes is truly one of triumph and tragedy.

The Rev. Thomas Knox Magee Morrow, Shaftesbury's Turbulent Priest

THE Rev. Thomas Knox Magee Morrow was appointed rector of the parishes of Holy Trinity and St. Peter's, Shaftesbury, in October 1870. The patron was the Earl of Shaftesbury, who at that time was the seventh earl, the great philanthropist. This appointment was to prove a disaster and led to over eight years of continual strife between the parson and his parishioners.

When it was known who the new incumbent was to be and his background, without doubt there would have been those who felt that he was not suitable for Shaftesbury; for he was an Ulsterman and a former

Rev T K M Morrow

Presbyterian. Many Shastonians would have looked upon him as a foreigner, also he had no experience of a rural parish. In fact he had only been ordained in 1862, when he was about forty-three years old. His previous ministry had been confined to two industrial parishes as curate of St. Paul's, Huddersfield and perpetual curate of St. James, Birkenhead. How he had conducted himself in these parishes is not known.

At the beginning of his time at Shaftesbury there were a few months of apparent harmony. Reports of the vestry meetings in 1871 show the parson, churchwardens and vestry members working together amicably on church matters. Nor was there any sign of discord when the Ancient Order of Foresters held their annual celebrations, which included a church parade when the rector had preached an excellent sermon and afterwards, at the feast, had responded to the toast to the bishop and clergy of the diocese. But the troubles were about to begin.

At Holy Trinity, he had dismissed the organist following a quarrel resulting in no music for several weeks. The Dowager Marchioness of Westminster, to whom most of Shaftesbury belonged, wrote a tactful letter to Lord Shaftesbury from her home at nearby Motcombe House, informing him of his appointee's conduct. She advised his Lordship that Morrow quarrelled with everyone and was using the pulpit to attack parishioners by name if they had offended him. Also, she complained that his sermons were too political and on occasions the Pope and Mr. Gladstone were subjected to verbal onslaughts. She stated that he was not a gentleman and that his wife was no lady and lacked the social graces.

Lord Shaftesbury, in his reply, expressed his deep distress and regret at the upset the reverend gentleman was causing but that he could do little to help. This was because a clergyman had the freehold of the living and could only be removed if he had committed a serious offence or was preaching heretical doctrine.

A deputation had gone to Salisbury to see the Bishop but again he could do little except perhaps to reprimand this troublesome priest.

But the Rev. Morrow was a fiery evangelical who believed he was doing right and that it was his duty to stay and fight the sinners at Shaftesbury and try and save them from hell and damnation.

Unfortunately the relationship between the rector and his parishioners continued to deteriorate. In 1873 the turbulent priest appeared in Shaftesbury Magistrates Court charged with assault on George Genge, Lady Westminster's land agent. In turn he brought a counter summons against Genge for assault. These offences were of a minor nature; grabbing hold of each other's coat collars and hurling abuse. The incident had taken place in a shop in the town where the rector had taken shelter from a mob who were hissing and booing him when Genge came in. It was then that the trouble began. In both cases the magistrates were unable to come to an agreed decision so there was no conviction. The quarrel had arisen because the rector had written in a pamphlet that some of the houses in the town were unfit to live in to which Genge had taken exception.

In the next month a local newspaper reported 'an extraordinary scene in church which occasioned much surprise and annoyance to the congregation. The Rev. Morrow, in announcing the text of his sermon, had dwelt significantly on the word 'drunkard' repeating it three times and apparently addressing his observations to Mr. F J Webb, who was seated in the body of the church and had just taken a very brief memorandum of the text. Suddenly stopping his discourse, the preacher exclaimed, pointing to Webb 'Clerk turn that man out of church or bring him up here'. Both the clerk and the sexton hastened to obey the imperious mandate but the accused would not move. This extraordinary scene lasted some minutes. Mr. Morrow then exclaimed 'Then I shall close the service' and having uttered a long and significant prayer, he pronounced the Benediction and closed the service'. The newspaper also commented that such an occurrence in a Christian church is indecent and an outrage that ought never to occur again.

Later that month the reverend gentleman was once more in court, charged with assaulting a choirboy. Again the assault was a minor one and again there was a counter summons by the defendant who claimed he had been subjected to some bad behaviour by the boy. The result was that the rector lost and was fined one shilling and costs. He had previously withdrawn his case against the boy as a gesture of goodwill but his opponents were not prepared to reciprocate.

It was in July of the same year that the unfortunate rector made his first appearance in the County Court. The case was brought by his former Curate for underpayment of his stipend, the amount being four pounds one shilling. Although the Judge gave the litigants an opportunity to settle the matter out of court, Morrow refused and wanted the case to be heard which resulted in him losing and having to pay the amount claimed and costs.

The year 1874 did not start well for him either. In January he was fined for assault on the waywarden whom he had accused of deliberately off-loading flintstones in front of the rectory and in an effort to move the horse, which was resisted by the waywarden who in consequence suffered an injury to his hand. This resulted in the defendant being bound over to keep the peace for six months. In the following month the unfortunate clergyman incurred the wrath of Mr. Bennett-Stanford, a local landowner and the Conservative candidate for Shaftesbury in the election, for canvassing for his opponent the Liberal candidate. The clergy were expected to support the Conservatives and as Mr. Morrow did not Bennett-Stanford considered him a disgrace to the cloth.

Now it was the turn of the persecuted priest to get back at his enemies by bringing an action against George Genge and four other burgesses for using threatening language against him. The magistrates spent over three hours considering the case but decided in the end that it should be dismissed. As was usual for all cases involving the Rev. Morrow, the courtroom was packed.

In 1875, the fifth year of Thomas Morrow's ministry at Shaftesbury, the troubles however did not cease but were of a different nature and there were no court cases.

The annual vestry meetings brought their usual difficulties. The rector had absented himself from one meeting and it was unanimously agreed by those present that 'he deserved the most extreme censure that the meeting can possibly convey'. Not long after, a stone was thrown through a window at the rectory. In that year the unfortunate incumbent was blamed for the death of a baby because, it was alleged, he had refused to baptise the infant privately and that by taking it to church it had been taken ill due to the cold and died. But the coroner and jury did not agree and for once the rector was vindicated.

For the next four months all seemed quiet then it was the turn of the choir to complain. This was over the new chant books, which had been purchased from a special collection. The books had been marked by the clerk 'Not to be taken from the church' which had upset the choir. A deputation went to see the rector who supported the clerk. In consequence the choir went on strike. As the newspaper publishing this matter made no further reports, possibly because it had been considered by some as a storm in a teacup, the outcome is not known.

Holy Trinity Church, Shaftesbury

It seemed that 1876 was going to be peaceful at last but this was not to be. As the season of goodwill approached so did the advent of ill will in Shaftesbury, some of the rectory windows were smashed and the rector was manhandled in the street. His effigy was set alight and thrown against the rectory door. He had posters printed offering a reward of £10 if the perpetrators were named and successfully prosecuted but the bill poster was forbidden or strongly advised by some anonymous person not to display them. This person was most likely to have been Lady Westminster's agent, one of Morrow's enemies and greatly feared by most of the inhabitants of the town. This led to much correspondence in the *Western Gazette* extending over several weeks. A Mr. George Mitchell, who had Shaftesbury connections but lived in London, took up the cudgels in support of the beleaguered rector. Mitchell, in his letters, deplored the state of affairs in Shaftesbury and the persecution of a Christian minister by a clique led by Lady Westminster's agent but sadly there was no one who was prepared to mediate and the strife continued.

Actions for libel and slander were the next tactics to be used by the rector's opponents. In the summer of 1877 a libel action was brought by a former master of Shaftesbury Boys' school against the rector. Libellous remarks were made in a letter the rector had written to the Education Department, following the plaintiff's appointment to the headship of a school in London. The master had been subjected to abuse from the pulpit, being referred to as 'a man totally unfit to have the care and instruction of youth for he is an associate of mountebanks and frequenters of dram-shops and cricket fields'. Shaftesbury's rector seems to have been a puritan of the old school. The result was that the defendant had to pay £50 and costs.

The slander case was again the result of remarks made from the pulpit. The plaintiff was an architect and surveyor in the town whom the defendant had accused of deliberately trying to set fire to the rectory and when the two had met in the street the allegations had again been repeated and violent language had been used on both sides. In this case the defendant counter-claimed for slander and assault, but at the hearing they both agreed to withdraw their charges.

1878 was the last year of Thomas Morrow's time at Shaftesbury. It was a relatively quiet one but the 'clique' was still active. The Ancient Order of Foresters were persuaded to change their plans and not hold their service at Holy Trinity where the rector had agreed to preach. This led to correspondence in the local newspaper but, unusually for once, Morrow did not get involved. However he was involved in a case at the County Court when he was accused of overcharging for a burial. Typically of him he had not made any effort to seek a solution out of court and as usual the judgement was found for the plaintiff with costs.

Early in the following year the inhabitants of Shaftesbury were surprised and relieved to learn that their rector was leaving. It had all been kept very quiet but Lord Shaftesbury had written to Lady Westminster to inform her. His next parish was to be St. Philip's Fairfield in Liverpool, where he was to remain for twelve years.

Undoubtedly the chief cause of the dissension between the parson and his parishioners at Shaftesbury was his habit of abusing people from the pulpit. A correspondent to the local newspaper gave a description of what some of the preacher's actions were like when in the pulpit. On one occasion he brought his clenched fist down on the Bible and roared 'Listen to this ye cowards of Shaftesbury', thus causing nervous people to start in their seats. He was no respecter of persons, irrespective of rank. Lady Westminster herself, although not present, was at times subjected to 'unwarranted statements of abuse'. On another occasion, while standing in the street, he pointed to a man and shouted out'There is a man going to hell and dragging scores with him'.

But the Rev. Morrow did appeal to certain young people, although perhaps for the wrong reasons. Two teenage boys were overheard in conversation; 'Hello Bill bist gwaine to church?' 'I dunno' 'Come on, twill be a lark, old Morrow's sure to pitch into somebody'.

However the controversial parson did have some good points. He was an excellent preacher apart from his attacks on persons. He was concerned for the welfare of the poor and supported the agricultural workers in their efforts to obtain better wages, a fact that probably did not endear him to Lady Westminster's agent. He showed no servility to the nobility and gentry and was very critical of them. His patron was called 'the Poor Man's Earl' and the Rev. Morrow could have been called 'the Poor Man's Parson'.

He did however return to the South again to spend the last four years of his life from 1891-1895 as Rector of Barwick, a small parish near Yeovil. He was obviously highly thought of there as his obituary read: 'His kindly and benevolent disposition gained for him great esteem and affection and he will be keenly missed'.

Perhaps he had mellowed with age, or perhaps the environment of Barwick was more congenial for a priest of the Rev. Morrow's evangelical persuasion?

The Three Meshach Moores: Parish Clerks and Blacksmiths

THE blacksmith was once a prominent and respected member of the rural community and usually took an active part in local affairs. The forge also served as a meeting place where those who had horses to be shod or tools to be repaired chatted and gossiped while they waited for the job to be completed. They would be joined by others who had no particular business there but had just dropped in for a chat and in winter to enjoy the warmth of the hearth. To enable him to run his business the blacksmith had to read and write and keep accounts. This made him a suitable candidate for one of the several parish offices including that of the parish clerk. This was the most prestigious office because the appointment had to be approved by the bishop of the diocese and was generally for life.

The parish clerk was also paid, although the amount was modest. In addition he received a fee for baptisms and marriages. Another requirement was that he must be at least twenty years of age. There was also a preference for a married man. The parish clerk's duties included: preparing the church for services; arranging christenings; leading the congregation in the responses and in some churches completing the registers. The clerk therefore was the parson's right hand man and the second man in the parish church.

The Rev. William Barnes, the Dorset poet, called his old clerk at Whitcombe the 'Archbishop of York', because he used to say, with pride, to the young men who misbehaved in church, 'Now you 'ave a-got to mind I. I be the second man in the church – I be'.

In some parishes the clerk also performed the duties of the sexton for which he was also paid. These duties were: digging the graves and filling them in after a burial; taking care of the churchyard; cleaning the church and tolling the bell.

The north Dorset village of Motcombe provides an interesting example where three successive generations of the same family, grandfather, father and son were parish clerks and blacksmiths. They also, perhaps uniquely, had the same alliterative name of Meshach Moore.

The first Meshach was appointed parish clerk in 1822 following the death of the previous clerk, William Broadway, and the minute of the vestry to this effect is still extant.

Although he was the first generation of the Moore family to be appointed parish clerk, he was not the first to be a blacksmith. Meshach was the illegitimate son of Rachel Moore whose father was a blacksmith in Motcombe. There was also another forge in the village run by a member of the Moore family who was probably Meshach's uncle or cousin.

Although Motcombe appointed its own parish officers and fixed its poor rate, it formed part of the large ecclesiastical parish of Gillingham. Its church was, in fact, a chapel of ease and was served by curates who did not reside in the village. Fortunately, Meshach's home and smithy were situated very close to the church.

During the first Meshach's tenure of office, the First Marquess of Westminster had become Lord of the Manor. His eldest son, Earl Grosvenor, who resided at Motcombe House, was put in charge of the estate, which led to many improvements being made to the church and the parish.

The second Meshach succeeded his father when he died in 1838 and was to complete forty-seven years as parish clerk. About the time of his appointment, a new blacksmith arrived in the village and occupied a cottage within a stone's throw of Meshach's forge. He proceeded to build a forge there and commence business. His name was Robert Spinney, a member of an old family of blacksmiths who had their origins in Winterbourne Stickland. According to the 1851 census, the Spinneys were established as blacksmiths in seven north Dorset villages. They were Primitive Methodists and Motcombe was a Methodist stronghold with two chapels. Because he was a dissenter the new blacksmith would probably not have any work from the Lord of the Manor or the church but he would be assured of the custom of those of the same persuasion which included several of the farmers and tradesmen. There was, however, sufficient work to support all three and continued to do so for many years.

The second Meshach experienced many changes both in the church and the village during his long tenure of office. In 1843, a church was built at Enmore Green which then formed part of the ecclesiastical district of Motcombe. Although of great benefit to those in that area, it meant fewer marriage and christening fees for Meshach. A major change occurred three years later, when it was decided to pull down Motcombe church and build a new one on the same site, no doubt causing a great deal of disruption to the parish clerk in the execution of his duties; but the new church was completed within a year and was consecrated in July 1847.

By this time, Earl Grosvenor had succeeded his father as Marquess of Westminster and as Lord of the Manor. During his time Motcombe was extensively rebuilt. Meshach also benefited: he had a new house and smithy, which was built close to the site of the old one. A further improvement took place in 1860, when a house was built in the village for the curate, not far from the church. So at long last Motcombe had a curate in residence which made communication between clerk and curate much easier. However the time spent by the curates at Motcombe was of short duration: there were six within the space of twenty years, all in the second Meshach's period of office. The clerk would have to adapt to each curate and both were subject to criticism by Lady Westminster who had inherited the Motcombe estate on the death of the Marquess in 1869. On one occasion she complained that during the service they had run a race in the creed to see who could gabble to the end the quickest.

An event of great significance occurred in 1883, when Motcombe, with Enmore Green, became a separate ecclesiastical parish with its own vicar. The former curate's house was enlarged to provide suitable accommodation for the new incumbent and Enmore Green had its own curate. This meant that the parish clerk's status was also enhanced.

Meshach resigned his position two years before his death in 1877 at the age of seventy-seven. His gravestone in Motcombe churchyard proudly proclaims his long service, '47 years Clerk of Motcombe church'.

The status which the first two Meshachs had enjoyed was not to continue during the time of the last Meshach. Parish councils for civil parishes came into being in 1894 with their own clerk and elected councillors. They took over the parochial responsibilities from the church which was left to look after its own affairs. Nevertheless Meshach Moore continued to appear as parish clerk in the county directories.

Business at his forge appeared to be declining and the forge run by the other blacksmith named Moore closed down in the 1890s. The last Meshach's health had not been good for several years which led to his duties being performed by the deputy clerk who was also the sexton. After completing thirty-six years in office, the third Meshach resigned in December 1921. Had he continued for a further six months then the three generations would have completed a century of service as parish clerks of Motcombe.

After his death three years later there was no fourth Meshach to follow either at the forge or in the church. His only son, who had been called John Jesse, had died some years previously at the early age of thirty. There was however another Meshach Moore, the son of Meshach's brother Thomas, who was a blacksmith at Shaftesbury. Whether this Meshach followed his father's trade cannot be established.

The coming of the motor vehicle resulted in fewer horses being required. Spinney's forge closed in about 1923 but there was sufficient business for Meshach's successors to continue; one of whom, Arthur Thomas, on four occasions won the horse shoeing championship of Great Britain and numerous other awards in farriery competitions.

Meshach's forge, which had been built in 1857, continued to operate until 1997 when it, like so many other village smithies, closed down.

The Forge in the third Mesnach Moore's time

The Rev. Canon John Smith: Motcombe's First Vicar 1883–1892

UNTIL 1883 Motcombe was part of the large ecclesiastical parish of Gillingham. This meant that its parish church and vicar were there and its present church was only a chapel with a curate in charge.

When the Vicar of Gillingham died in 1882, the Dowager Marchioness of Westminster, who owned the Motcombe estate and was a regular worshipper at Motcombe chapel, used her powerful influence and wealth to persuade the Bishop of Salisbury to make Motcombe with Enmore Green, which had been in a similar situation, into a separate parish. Her request was granted. She also intimated whom she would like to have as the vicar, namely, the Rev. Canon John Smith who was the Vicar of Lyme Regis but had been Rector of Kington Magna and Rural Dean of Shaftesbury. She undertook to contribute £200 per annum to his stipend and to have the former curate's house (now called The Old Rectory) considerably enlarged.

Canon Smith accepted the offer and so became Motcombe's first vicar commencing his duties at the end of 1883.

The reasons why the 86 years old Dowager Marchioness had been keen to have Canon Smith at Motcombe was because he was an excellent preacher who preached in language that was understood by all as well as being a conscientious and devoted parish priest.

During his time the attendance at church greatly improved. One very popular event was the annual flower service when the children brought bunches of flowers and presented them to Lady Westminster. They were then sent to Shaftesbury Hospital and to one of the London Hospitals for sick children, where a ward was named after Motcombe.

In 1891 Canon Smith and his wife suffered the sad loss of their daughter, Lucy, aged 23, who had lived with them. Just two months later Lady Westminster died aged 94 when he officiated and preached a very befitting sermon at her funeral.

In the following year he retired to live at Shaftesbury, occasionally returning to Motcombe to officiate at a baptism, wedding or funeral, always completing the registers in his beautiful copperplate handwriting.

He died in 1904 at the age of 79. His wife had predeceased him in 1898. He was buried in Motcombe churchyard with his wife and daughter, where his headstone can still be seen on the south side of the church near the chancel. The wording on the headstone aptly describes him as an 'earnest and zealous worker for Christ during a long and useful life'.

Three Motcombe Sisters and Several Carpenters

A NNA, Ellen and Sarah were the three daughters of John and Martha Arnold. John, a carpenter, died when his children were still young. Martha then married Charles Green who kept a beer house which, when rebuilt, became the present Royal Oak.

Anna, born in 1830, married William Pitman, not a carpenter but two of their thirteen children were to follow that trade. At first William and Anna lived at Knapp. When No. 65, at the top of Elm Hill was built, they moved there and started a bakery and grocery business.

Motcombe Post Office, about 1906

Ellen married Thomas Parsons, also a carpenter, son of John Parsons, carpenter and builder. Later they kept a shop and then the Post Office (now the Old Post House). The shop, long since gone, was next to the Post Office.

Sarah married John Broadway, another carpenter and son of Edward Broadway, yet another carpenter and builder. When Sarah's parents died Sarah and John took over the Royal Oak.

Perhaps all this seems rather remote, but by adding that William and Anna were the late Gwen Palmer's grand¬parents and that Thomas and Ellen were the same for the late Claude Stainer, it certainly adds much interest. This, of course, made Gwen and Claude second cousins.

John Broadway: a Man of Sorrows

JOHN Broadway was born at Motcombe on 15 October 1835, one of the ten children of Edward Broadway, a carpenter and builder, and his wife Ann.

The Broadways at that time did not enjoy the same status as earlier generations of their family who had been considered to be lesser gentry. The imposing table tomb in the front of Motcombe church for William and Frances Broadway and some of their fourteen children is evidence of their former prosperity and social standing.

William and Frances were Edward Broadway's great-grandparents. Some of their large family became Methodists and used their wealth to build chapels in the area and give generous financial support to further the Methodist cause.

The former Royal Oak Hotel at Motcombe

Edward was a Methodist and a trustee of the Primitive Methodist chapel at Motcombe. There was already a Wesleyan Methodist chapel in the village in which members of the Broadway family had also been actively involved.

John Broadway followed his father in his trade but, although baptised and brought up a Methodist, appears not to have continued in that persuasion as all his children were baptised in Motcombe parish church.

In 1856 he married Sarah Arnold, the youngest of the three daughters of John and Martha Arnold. John, who was also a carpenter, had died of consumption when Sarah was only three. Her mother had then married Charles Green who kept 'The Royal Oak' a beer house at Motcombe which Martha took over after her husband's death. Following her death in 1866, John Broadway became the licensee, combining this with his other trade, although it is possible that his wife managed the beer house.

By that time John and Sarah had had four children and in 1868 their fifth child was born. In the following year they suffered their first loss when nine year old Kate died from broncho-pneumonia. Twelve months later a new 'Royal Oak', the present building, was built close to the old one which was pulled down. John Broadway was the builder and also became the licensee.

It was a superior building for a small village as Motcombe then was. It was three storeys in height with six bedrooms and four attic rooms. Some of these rooms were intended for guests, hence it was known as 'The Royal Oak Hotel'. The Broadways now had a spacious new home with all the modern conveniences of that period. Unfortunately, however, it was to bring much sadness.

Their sixth child was born in 1871, a son, Edward John, who survived only eight months. The cause of death, according to the death certificate, was 'Dentition and Convulsions'. Two years later, Sarah died from consumption, the disease that had killed her father. She was thirty-eight.

Within the space of four months, John was again bereaved when his seventh and youngest child, Edith Kate, an infant of eighteen months died from atrophy indicating, perhaps, that she had lacked proper care after the illness and then loss of her mother. Only one day after Edith's funeral John's father died. There is no entry of his burial in the Motcombe church register so it is assumed that he was interred in the small graveyard at the Primitive Methodist chapel.

There seemed to be no end to John's sorrows. A year had not elapsed before he was again bereaved when his thirteen year old daughter Frances died of tubercular meningitis. He had now lost four of his seven children.

On 29 January 1876 the once-widowed John Broadway, then aged forty, married the twice-widowed Louisa Scammell, aged thirty-nine. Her previous husband had been a Motcombe farmer and considerably older than her. She had had two children by her first marriage, a son and a daughter. The son was later to marry John Broadway's eldest daughter Sarah. Before the year was out Louisa died of broncho-pneumonia. The date of her decease was 2 December 1876, ten months and three days after their marriage. She was laid to rest in the same grave as John's first wife in Motcombe churchyard where their headstone can still be seen.

Now with the loss of two wives and four children, this unfortunate man decided to give up as licensee of 'The Royal Oak' and begin a new life at West Knoyle, a village about six miles from Motcombe, to take up farming at Broadmead Farm. The date of his departure cannot be ascertained but was most probably either in 1877 or 1878. By then his eldest daughter Sarah had married his step-son Charles Ricketts, his other daughter, Eliza, was fourteen and his only surviving son, Isaac, ten.

It was at West Knoyle that Farmer Broadway married for a third time, his new bride was Laura Harriet Parsons. The date of their wedding was 21 April 1879 and they were both aged forty-three. This marriage lasted seven years when Laura died following an apoplectic stroke.

Fifteen months later on 12 January 1888 John married for the fourth and last time, Sarah White. She was forty-eight and John by then was fifty-two. This marriage did last sixteen years, a few months shorter than his first. The cause of Sarah's demise, which occurred on 22 May 1904, was 'Enteritis Intestinal Obstruction and Peritonitis'.

This veritable man of sorrows was to survive a further six years, when he himself died of 'Old Age

Sarah and Louisa Broadway's headstone in Motcombe churchyard

and Heart Disease' at the age of seventy-six.

To lose four wives, although very exceptional, was not unique. Only a few miles away the Rev. John Wyndham, Rector of Sutton Mandeville, who died in 1897, had also lost four wives.

One consolation for John was that his three surviving children, who also would have been traumatised by the loss of their mother and siblings, grew up, married and had children whom John lived long enough to see.

Thanks to the great advance of medical science and improved living conditions, the maladies which caused the early deaths of eight members of a family of twelve, would not, in all probability, have done so today.

Nehemiah Arnold was Father Christmas

I T is pleasing that, despite the sophisticated age in which we live, Father Christmas has survived, although the age at which children disbelieve is probably earlier than it was nearly eighty years ago.

One young Motcombe lad at that time was an early doubter, finding it difficult to accept that Father Christmas existed. Having been told by his parents that none of them dressed up as Father Christmas, he concluded that it must be Nehemiah Arnold. Nehemiah, usually called 'Neemy', lived with Mr and Mrs Jack Lear at 48 The Street. He was very old with a long grey beard and therefore ideally suited for that role.

The young lad when going to Haydens (the village shop) would sometimes see Neemy leaning on the gate, his long grey beard hanging over it. The more the lad saw the old man, the more convinced he became that Nehemiah was Father Christmas. One day he was told that old Mr Arnold had 'gone to Heaven'. He was quite perturbed. How inconsiderate of him to do that before Christmas! It looked as if there would be no presents now. So he decided it would be better to believe again – and, of course, Father Christmas came. Nehemiah Arnold died in 1933 at the age of eighty-seven. He was one of the children of James and Mansel Arnold who lived at 35 The Street next to Barn House (opposite the Memorial Hall). He worked at Motcombe factory until he was over eighty.

Charles Prideaux (1852–1940) Entrepreneur: From Railwayman's Cottage to Country Mansion

IN the second half of the nineteenth century there were three men in Motcombe who through success in their respective businesses put this north Dorset village on the map. Two of them, Arthur Hiscock and Nathaniel Benjafield, have already been the subjects of an article in a previous edition of the *Dorset Year Book*. The third was Charles Prideaux, a contemporary of Arthur and Nathaniel, who achieved fame through his entrepreneurial and inventive skills with dairy produce.

The Prideauxs were originally a Cornish family, but during the course of the centuries they dispersed far and wide. Charles' branch of the family settled in the Barnstaple area of Devon, where they were occupied mainly in trade but his father, William, was a railway porter, and later a signalman, at Umberleigh station near Barnstaple. His mother, Sarah, was a nurse. They lived in a railway cottage where they raised a family of seven; Charles was the eldest son and the second child.

Little information now exists on his childhood days, but it is known that he developed a flair for business at an early age. While still at school he delivered telegrams and canvassed orders for a coal merchant who, on one recorded occasion, must have been very pleased with young Charles when he received four orders in one day, one of which was for five hundredweight.

After leaving school at the age of twelve he began work as a messenger boy at Barnstaple station telegraph office, where the precocious Charles soon learnt to operate the telegraph and became combined telegraph operator and ticket clerk. Conscious of his age and height the young railway clerk wore a bowler hat and stood on a box behind the ticket window. His pay was ten shillings a week, but the enterprising young clerk now saw a golden opportunity to earn some extra money: he started making gingerbeer and selling it in the waiting room, realising a small profit.

Charles was conscious that the schooling he had had was inadequate for one who wished to get on in the world. He therefore began to educate himself by reading widely and studying books on subjects which he felt would be of use to him.

By the time he was eighteen the ticket clerk and gingerbeer maker had left his native Devon and was working as a goods clerk at Semley station which was on the main line between London and Exeter. It served too as the station for Shaftesbury. This move must have been by way of promotion; for his salary was now one hundred pounds per annum. He lodged nearby in the home of one of the porters. The gingerbeer making enterprise of his Barnstaple days was now superseded, when he had sufficient money, by buying and selling potatoes. He bought a load and sold them piecemeal and also earned extra money by keeping the account books of a local businessman.

It was during his Semley days that he began his rounds, visiting farms to buy eggs, an after work activity which entailed walking up to ten miles in all weathers, and depending on the season, sometimes in the dark. This could be regarded as Charles' form of recreational activity. He appears not to have participated in any sport; when once asked what his hobbies were, his reply was 'Work.' Nor did he ever, throughout his life, take a holiday. It was probably on his rounds that he met his future wife, Veronica Harrison, the daughter of an East Knoyle farmer whom he married in 1876. She proved to be a great help to her enterprising husband, particularly in the early days, working together, sometimes to midnight, making boxes and packing eggs.

Charles Prideaux got sufficient capital to start his own business in an unusual way: by buying the gate at Semley fête and pony races on two successive occasions. This was a popular annual event and could, on a good day, attract up to three thousand entrants. It appears that on both occasions the weather to begin with was not propitious, but later, greatly improved, thus attracting considerably more people than had been anticipated, resulting in a profit for Charles on the two events of seventy pounds. So his gamble had paid off; thus enabling him to use part of the proceeds to buy a pony and cart so that he could cover a wider area and buy butter as well as eggs.

It is not known where the Prideaux's first home was but in 1878 they moved to Motcombe and rented a cottage belonging to the Motcombe estate. The rent was seven pounds per annum. In the latter part of the following year Charles decided to give up his job with the railway which offered security, good prospects and a pension, and start up a business on his own. It was a very risky step to take; no wonder that his father did not approve.

The novice businessman now went to London as often as he could to sell his butter and eggs. The buyers informed him that they were not satisfied with the butter because it varied in colour and quality. Realizing that there would be a good market for butter of uniform colour and quality, he and his younger brother George, who had now joined him, began the process of blending it and claimed to be the first to do so. In later years Prideauxs bought butter in large quantities from New Zealand for blending. It was shipped in wooden boxes with the firm's name and 'Motcombe, Dorset' stamped on each box.

Initially the two brothers did the blending manually. It was hard and monotonous work. Between them they would beat up, with wooden mallets, between five and six hundredweight a day. The blended butter sold well and the quantities proved too much for the manual process, so a blending machine was invented. It was a primitive affair drawn by a horse walking in a circle and harnessed to a beam. By this time the Prideauxs had moved to a larger cottage in Motcombe with an acre of ground thus affording room for expansion. The butter business continued to increase with advertisements appearing regularly in local newspapers requesting butter 'In lump from churn not made or salted' with 'baskets and cloths supplied free'. These advertisements resulted in butter arriving from further afield so the horse drawn contraption became obsolete and a steam engine was installed.

A provision business was the next venture dealing in poultry, game and general agricultural products. Pigs were bought, killed and made into bacon and sausages. Cheese too was made in large quantities. Then came milk and a small creamery was built opposite the Prideauxs' cottage and George Prideaux was put in charge. Cream followed, which initially came from two Jersey cows kept in a two acre field nearby. This venture too proved to be a great success.

Charles Prideaux's crowning achievement and perhaps the most profitable came, after much experimenting, in making edible casein from separated milk. The product was called 'Casumen'. In 1900 the two brothers formed a company with the ponderous name of Prideaux Pure Casein and Milk Food Company Ltd. to market this product, which was advertised extensively extolling its medicinal properties. Government contracts were won to supply the War Office for use in military hospitals. Two years later the same steam-heated cylinders employed in making 'Casumen' were used to produce dried milk powder. The two Prideauxs claimed to be pioneers of casein and dried milk products. During the First World War a full cream milk powder was first made and marketed under the brand name of 'Dorsella'. On 1 August 1914 the company of C & G Prideaux Ltd. was incorporated. It was a private limited company with all the shares being held by members of the family. Charles Prideaux, of course, was chairman and kept firm control of the operations of both companies. That year too, saw the opening of the last of the creameries at Wanstrow in Somerset. They now totalled eight. The others were, besides Motcombe, Stalbridge [1892], Shillingstone

Prideaux's milk factory, about 1906

[1897], and Evercreech [1900]. This creamery had been bought from the Maypole Dairy Company. Mere [1907], Lydlinch and Castle Cary [1910]. These creameries were operated under C & G Prideaux Ltd. while the provision, bacon and poultry business traded as Charles Prideaux.

The advent of the Great War meant many changes: increased business due to Government contracts and jobs being taken over by women when the men were called up. After the war and the return of his men the boss invited all the Motcombe employees to a meeting in the factory to hear details of the working both financial and otherwise of the business. Like most employers at that time he was worried about the advance of trade unionism and the danger to the country and, of course, his own business, of trouble between capital and labour. Cheques representing ten per cent of each person's wages were given to all members of staff which numbered about a hundred. To every ex-serviceman who had returned to his job a cheque for five pounds was given. However there were no industrial troubles in the Prideaux firm.

In the 1920s Charles Prideaux took advantage of Government subsidies to provide his Motcombe employees with new houses. No fewer than twenty-six were built containing all the modern conveniences for that period and with large gardens.

His last enterprise was begun in 1930 when nearly eighty. It was cider making. There were numerous apple orchards in Motcombe and before the war much cider had been made mainly for home consumption; but after 1918 this had considerably decreased resulting in large quantities of apples being left to rot. Charles the entrepreneur saw an opportunity to make profitable use of them. So they were bought from the farmers and in the first year twenty thousand gallons of cider were made.

Shortly after his eightieth birthday the former messenger boy granted an interview to a national newspaper. when he proudly gave some statistical details of the business and his achievements, which included the following: by 1914 the milk business amounted to ten thousand gallons a day; during the war the turnover of his combined businesses reached about one million pounds a year; his workforce at that time totalled two hundred; there were forty lorries and the transport costs amounted to thirty thousand pounds a year; he had his own printing works at Gillingham Dorset where all the packaging for his products was made. The article concluded with the reasons for his success which he attributed to hard thinking, concentrating on the thing in hand and trying by foresight to see the end before starting on a new venture.

Charles Prideaux died at his home on 4 January 1940 shortly after his eighty-seventh birthday having maintained to the end a lively interest in his business affairs. The funeral took place two days later on a Saturday afternoon. After the factory had closed at midday the employees went home, put on their funeral clothes, and assembled outside the Prideaux's home to head the large cortege through the

Retirement of Glyn Stone from Motcombe factory in 1959 after 57 years' service; presentation by Lionel Prideaux

village street. Motcombe, quiet and peaceful in those days, was even quieter than usual. Muffled touches were rung on the church bells and all the blinds and curtains were drawn in the houses along the route. On arrival at the church the employees formed a guard of honour when the coffin, borne by six long serving employees, was taken into the crowded church. After the service a guard of honour was again formed from the church to the grave, which was surrounded by a mass of floral tributes, where the former railway clerk turned successful entrepreneur was laid to rest.

The Subsequent History of C. & G. Prideaux Ltd

GEORGE Prideaux, thirteen years his brother's junior, became head of the business after Charles's death. When only twenty-three he had been put in charge of the creamery at Motcombe which had opened in 1888. Following his marriage in 1892 he moved to Stalbridge to take charge of the newly opened creamery. As the number two in the business he had been much involved in its development, having assisted his brother, who was very much the dominant partner, in building it up to become one of the largest undertakings of its kind in South West England.

It was during his time that, in 1945, the Cow and Gate Group acquired a controlling interest in the business and the casein company's ponderous name was simplified to Prideaux Milk Foods Ltd. Four years later George Prideaux died at the age of eighty-four and was succeeded by his son Lionel, who had joined the business in 1915. He had been a director for many years working at the Head Office at Motcombe. His son, Peter, also became engaged in the business in 1955 as manager of the Motcombe factory. The Cow & Gate Group acquired full control of the Prideaux companies in 1959 and in 1967 the Prideaux name ceased to exist when the business was sold to Case & Son Ltd.

Charles Prideaux's Children

CHARLES and Veronica Prideaux had five children: two sons and three daughters. The eldest son William was born a year after their arrival at Motcombe and tragically died of rheumatic fever in 1897 at the age of eighteen. He had begun working for his father by assisting in the office and it was said that he had shown great promise of becoming a sound man of business.

The other four children Mabel, Ethel, Dora and Henry all grew up to occupy responsible positions in the business. The three daughters each held secretarial posts. Their proud father contended that, although he had tried other secretaries, they did not compare with his daughters. They did not marry; in their father's eyes no suitor was good enough for them.

Henry had charge of the milk contracts and developed the bacon business. After his marriage he moved to Mere and like his cousin, Lionel, travelled to Motcombe each day. He had four children, three sons Dudley, Humphrey and Beville and one daughter, Joan. Dudley and Humphrey occupied positions in the business for a time. After it was acquired by the Cow and Gate Group all Charles' family moved to Bournemouth.

Charles Prideaux at 85

The Upward Mobility of Charles Prideaux

As Charles Prideaux's business grew so did his status in the local community and beyond. Ten years after he had set up on his own, not only does his name appear in the commercial section of *Kelly's Directory*, but was also included in the private residents section along with the nobility, gentry and principal personages in the village. The funeral of his eldest son in 1897 provided further evidence of his rise in the class-conscious society of that time. Over one hundred telegrams of condolence were received including one from Lord Stalbridge, the owner of the Motcombe estate , and the Bishop of Salisbury. Sixty-seven employees attended the funeral, together with most of Motcombe's farmers and tradesmen.

Three years later, probably feeling that his home was not commensurate with his present status, Charles decided to build a new one on a two acre site opposite. Some of the stone from the old Motcombe House, which had been demolished, was used in the construction. The facade closely followed that of the old mansion but on a much smaller scale. The new house, called 'The Grange', was quite an imposing residence and much in keeping with the standing of its owner..

Charles Prideaux suffered the sad loss of his wife in 1923. Nothing is now known how the one time farmer's daughter felt about the status she shared with her husband. The fact that she had been an invalid in the latter years of her life would have been sufficient reason for her to have opted out of the social round; a role she delegated to her daughters. In life she had been able to shun the limelight; but in death she had no choice: she was given a grand funeral.

Lord Stalbridge's Motcombe estate was sold in 1925, when Charles Prideaux took the opportunity of buying some of the cottages and farms. The cottages were modernised and became homes for his workers. After the sale Lord Stalbridge left Motcombe for good, leaving Charles Prideaux as the principal property owner and the largest employer. So he was now virtually the new squire. However, he still lacked one important item – Motcombe House – the squire's residence, which had not been sold in 1925 and in 1929, was threatened with demolition.

The Grange as it was in Charles Prideaux's time

The entrepreneurial squire made an offer for it which was accepted. His first home had been a railwayman's cottage; now he owned a country mansion. But the new owner did not occupy his palatial residence: it remained empty for ten years when it was let to a firm evacuated from London. Every Sunday afternoon, in his chauffeur driven Willys Knight saloon, and accompanied by one of his daughters, he would visit the empty mansion, look over it and return to The Grange, which was, by comparison, a modest home.

Charles Prideaux: the Man

CHARLES Prideaux was a typical Victorian employer, autocratic. paternalistic, feared but respected by his workforce, all of whom he knew by name, regarding them as members of his business family. It was easy to be sacked; but easy to be re-instated provided assurances were given that the offence would not be repeated. On more than one occasion the assurances were given by the offender's mother. Her son had a weakness for visiting 'The Royal Oak' nearby during working hours and had been found out. Perhaps he had been absent when 'the old man' had made his daily rounds; he had the habit of varying his times for obvious reasons. However everyone knew when the boss was around because his approach was announced by the smell of his cigar.

Some Motcombe factory workers at the Royal Oak, about 1960

Almost to the end of his long life 'the old man' would, on occasions, take a walk in the village; a very distinguished figure, tall and erect despite his age and usually wearing a button-hole. In fact, every inch a country gentleman who would pass the time of day with those he met; smile benevolently at a child and ask his or her name and on one remembered occasion, encourage two small children to run a race, rewarding the winner with a penny.

Charles Prideaux did much good in Motcombe, like his brother at Stalbridge; he was active in local affairs serving as a churchwarden; a parish councillor; a school manager and acting as treasurer on several committees. It was due to his efforts that a fine village hall was built in memory of the first Lord Stalbridge whom he greatly revered. He took a particular interest in the Motcombe Nursing Association, giving it financial support and providing the district nurse with a home.

Over seventy years have now elapsed since his death and naturally there have been many changes. The Grange has now been converted into retirement homes and the factory site a housing estate.

Charles Prideaux and Motcombe Factory in the days of C. & G. Prideaux Ltd

THERE are still a few Motcombe people who can remember the days before the last war when the farmers took the milk to the factory by horse and cart where the churns were off-loaded on to the stage and the contents emptied into a long trough. The churns were then steam-washed by Charles Arnold and rolled back on to the cart.

Motcombe people could buy milk from the factory as it was sold retail as well as wholesale. Children, when old enough, usually had the job of getting it. There were no bottles then so cans were used. Harold Lear was the man to see. He filled the can by dipping the milk up from a churn. He also gave you a ticket for the quantity which you took to Stanley Beacham in the office and paid him.

One of the people working in the office was Billy Meadows. He was always smartly dressed and wore spats. He also rode an auto-cycle to work from his home at Knapp.

You could buy excellent cream from Prideaux's as well. This was made by Jack Clark and Tilly Coward. Originally it was sold in small stone jars but later in tins.

Prideaux's was very much a family business with Charles Prideaux the head and his four children, one son and three daughters holding responsible positions in the company. They were referred to as Mr. Henry, Miss Mabel, Miss Ethel and Miss Dora. There was Mr. Lionel too, who was also a director. He lived at Stalbridge and came to Motcombe every day by car. His father was George Prideaux, the 'G' in C & G Prideaux, and was head of the Stalbridge factory.

A person who had to work on Sundays was Guy Mead. During the week he drove one of the Dennis lorries, but on Sundays he was Charles Prideaux's chauffeur when, wearing his chauffeur's uniform he drove his boss and his three daughters to church on Sunday mornings in a smart Willys Knight saloon; and in the afternoon drove him to look over his empty mansion, Motcombe House (now Port Regis School) in which he and his family never lived. While there he probably contrasted this with his humble beginnings in a railwayman's cottage in Devonshire, before returning to his more modest yet spacious home 'The Grange' next to his factory.

Arthur Hiscock 1858–1936: a Famous Dorset Farmer and Stockbreeder

ARTHUR Hiscock was a celebrated Dorset farmer and stockbreeder renowned by agriculturists throughout the world for his pedigree cattle and pigs. His life ended at Church Farm Child Okeford on 20 May 1936 but coincidentally it had begun at another Church Farm at West Stour where he and his twin sister Harriet were born on 21 September 1858, the youngest of the nine children of Arthur and Harriet Hiscock. Very little is known of Arthur's childhood. There was no school at West Stour until 1872. Before that time the children went to East Stour and it is probable that the young Arthur did so too. It is known that later he was a pupil at Bourton Academy near Gillingham,

Arthur Hiscock

but no dates or information on his academic record have survived. This establishment was a boarding and day school for young gentlemen according to an advertisement, and catered for boys between the ages of ten and fourteen.

Sometime in the 1870s, Arthur Hiscock senior moved to a larger farm at West Stour, Manor Farm, leaving one of his sons as tenant of Church Farm. A further move in 1882 was to be a significant one for Arthur Hiscock junior, when his father took over the tenancy of Manor Farm, Motcombe, again a larger farm of about 260 acres. Moreover it was relatively modern having been rebuilt in 1836 following a fire. The farmhouse was spacious and the farm buildings were well constructed providing good accommodation for the farm stock. This farm was part of the Motcombe estate and adjoined the Park in which Motcombe House was situated. This was the home of the Lady of the Manor, the Dowager Marchioness of Westminster noted for her generosity and her concern for the welfare of her tenants.

Three years later young Arthur Hiscock married Mary, daughter of Charles Williams of North End Farm, Motcombe. The wedding was a grand affair with four bridesmaids and numerous guests contrasting sharply with the weddings of farm labourers in those days who often had to beg for time off and usually had to return to work directly after the ceremony. Following their honeymoon at Torquay the couple returned to live at Manor Farm with Arthur's parents but not for long, the older Hiscocks retired soon after leaving their son as tenant and thus free to pursue his ambitions.

When Arthur junior took over there was only one animal eligible for the Herd Book: a bull called 'Gazelle Duke'. Owning this animal was one of the principal reasons which prompted him to set about forming a pedigree herd. He therefore began to attend sales of Shorthorns throughout the country so that eventually with purchases and breeding the famous herd of Manor Farm Shorthorns numbered 133. It was not however with pedigree cattle that Arthur gained his initial success but with crossbred pigs, which he entered at the Smithfield Club show in 1882. This was the same year that the Hiscocks had arrived at Motcombe, when his father was still the tenant, thus proving that the enterprising young farmer had lost no time in realising his ambition to exhibit at major shows. The prize was in a class for single pigs and was the first of thousands that he would win over the next forty years.

By 1888, he had made great progress, leading a local newspaper to comment: 'It must be gratifying to a young exhibitor like Arthur Hiscock junior to have again met with phenomenal success at Smithfield show with a pen of white pigs less than twelve months. He not only won the first prize in the class but the still higher honour by being reserved for the £20 championship for the best pen of pigs of any breed in the show.' Reports such as this were to be a regular feature in the local press and sometimes in the national papers following his ever-increasing successes in shows throughout the country. The crossbred pigs were later to be superseded by pedigree Berkshires, Large and Middle Whites and Yorkshires.

In the 1890s his Shorthorn cattle were making the headlines. Bulls with names such as 'Manor Victor', 'Manor Invaluable' and a fine stud bull 'Sevastopol' were receiving much publicity and the top awards. At the Birmingham show in 1900, a bull which had won first prize was sold for 200 guineas and exported to Buenos Aires. Both his cattle and pigs were now being shipped to all parts of the world and Manor Farm had become a mecca for pedigree cattle and pig buyers including representatives of British and Foreign Royalty. Arthur had not only achieved fame himself but had also put Motcombe on the map.

The sales at Manor Farm were grand occasions. Luncheon was provided by professional caterers in a large marquee; prospective buyers were conducted round the various pens to see the animals all, of course, in tip-top condition. Also there would be an opportunity to see cheese being made. The whey from the cheese tub, so Arthur contended, combined with strict attention to the feeding and comfort of the pigs, were prime factors for securing success in the showyard. At one time one could witness the famous cow 'Kirklevington Fillpail' being milked. This illustrious animal yielded four gallons of milk weighing 41½ lbs at a milking.

By the beginning of the last century Arthur had become the tenant of two more farms: Church Farm at Motcombe and Church Farm at Child Okeford. Manor Farm Motcombe continued to be the Hiscock's home where callers were always made most welcome; for the master was noted for his unstinted hospitality which meant that whisky, the host's favourite liquid refreshment, would be freely available and also cider made from apples from his orchards for those who preferred it.

Had not Arthur found fame as a champion cattle and pig breeder, he would surely have done so as an entertainer; he was the life and soul at social functions, concerts and parties. His cheery nature, combined with his talent as a singer and story teller, would have his audience in fits of laughter or, as a newspaper report once put it, 'Mr. Hiscock convulsed the audience with his mirth-provoking themes.' His repertoire included country songs such as 'Hurrah for the life of a Farmer' which ended with a rousing 'Cock-a-doodle-doo'. This was one of the songs he sang at a Smithfield Club lunch in a year when he had done extremely well having won the supreme championship in the pig section. Two of the Berkshires had been declared the best pair ever seen at a Smithfield show. No wonder that this renowned showman was in a particularly jubilant mood that day. To add to his joy, King George V had stopped at his pen to congratulate him. Arthur was no stranger to royalty – he had once received a gold pig charm from King Edward VII – on this occasion the excited farmer gripped both His Majesty's hands and made an impassioned speech to the highly amused Monarch; 'You are the best man in Great Britain today. Your father was the best man who ever lived and your grandmother was superb and sweet'. He then called for round after round of cheers. The King, it was reported, thoroughly enjoyed the occasion.

On that day too, Dan Travers the Manor Farm pigman had the honour of being presented. Dan had attended thirty-four shows at Smithfield and had been in Arthur's employ for nearly forty years. When the King heard this he exclaimed 'Well done good and faithful servant' and shook him warmly by the hand.

It was one of Arthur's proud boasts that he was a good employer, a boast borne out by the length of service of his employees. As regards the good and faithful servant, it must have been so, to have retained his services for so long. It was said that it was also due to Dan's knowledge and skills that his master had been able to achieve so much. With such a competent man left in charge, it was easier for Arthur to be absent to attend shows the length and breadth of the country in another capacity: that of a show judge. This involved not only judging at the showground, but visiting entrants within a given radius of the showground site, when there was a competition for the dairy herd. This was time consuming and exhausting. In addition a detailed report had to be submitted to the show authorities. Fortunately Judge Hiscock was endowed with much physical stamina. On occasions he had to travel great distances to the showgrounds and after a busy day would return home very late at night but would invariably be up early the following morning ready for the day's work.

His physical stamina had served him well when as a young man he had been a notable athlete winning trophies for pole jumping; walking; running and penny-farthing bicycle racing. In 1880, according to a newspaper report, he had run a mile on the flat in four minutes seven seconds. Again he thrived on competition and loved a contest which, needless to say, he usually won, leaving his contestants lighter in pocket.

However on one occasion he was not so fortunate. This was with a horse race when he challenged a farmer friend to a race over two miles.

The stake was two pounds to the winner. Arthur was in the lead until the last lap when his competitor took the lead and won by seven lengths.

There were setbacks too with his animals but nothing compared with the great disaster which he suffered in 1914 due to an outbreak of swine fever at his Manor Farm resulting in the compulsory destruction of his entire herd of pedigree pigs numbering 136. The herd was considered to be the best in Great Britain. It was a devastating blow too for another reason: the financial loss which was estimated at about £2000. In addition large quantities of whey would have been wasted during the isolation period. Compensation from the Board of Agriculture was limited to £20 for a pedigree animal, which was quite inadequate considering that the owner had recently refused an offer of eighty guineas for a sow. Whether the Board of Agriculture made an exception in this case is not known, bearing in mind that the loser had done so much to raise the standard and value of pigs in the country.

Arthur was not a man to be crushed by this blow. He was greatly heartened by the messages of support he received from far and wide. Fortunately all was not lost: he had his young stock at his Child Okeford farm which was unscathed. This enabled him to rebuild his herd and to exhibit at the Smithfield show in the following December albeit on a reduced scale.

The Manor Farm, Motcombe, Arthur Hiscock's home

The First World War ended in 1918, but a conflict of a different kind began at Motcombe in the following year. It was a bloodless one and on a personal level between Arthur Hiscock [tenant] and Lord Stalbridge [landlord]. The dispute had arisen because the landlord had decided to raise the rents of his tenant farmers. Arthur was determined to oppose this and persuaded some other farmers to do the same, contending that if they presented a united front his Lordship would back down; but Arthur had underestimated his Landlord. Hugh, second Baron Stalbridge was totally unlike his father, an aristocrat of the old school, who in his Sunday afternoon walks, would call at Manor Farm, look at the prize animals and partake of his host's whisky.

His son Hugh however was a professional soldier, who had fought with distinction in both the South African and First World War and was awarded the Military Cross in the latter. He regarded the action of these recalcitrant farmers as insubordination and took stern measures to counteract it. The high standing of the leader in the locality and in the agricultural world made no difference, so this celebrated Motcombe farmer, who had played an active role in the local community for nearly forty years, was given notice to quit.

Arthur Hiscock therefore left Motcombe wearing the martyr's crown to take over the tenancy of Manor France Farm at Stourpaine, near Blandford on Viscount Portman's estate. On account of the move, Arthur had to give up most of his involvement in local affairs. During his time at Motcombe he had been a churchwarden; a school manager; a district councillor; a member of the Shaftesbury Board of Guardians and of Motcombe Parish Council, of which he had been chairman from 1906 to 1909. He continued as a committee member of the agricultural societies in the district and his membership of the prestigious national societies such as the Council of the British Berkshire Society; the Royal Counties Agricultural Society and the Royal Agricultural Society of England in which he represented Dorset for twenty-nine years.

Doubtless this colourful character made his presence felt at the meetings. On one occasion he definitely overstepped the mark. This was at Motcombe's Annual Parish Meeting in 1911 which was held that year at Enmore Green, then part of the parish of Motcombe. It had been agreed at a previous annual meeting to provide Motcombe with a club room, but now it was found that the cost would be substantially higher than had originally been anticipated. This led to a proposal to rescind the original agreement because Enmore Green ratepayers did not see why they should pay for a facility they would not benefit from, because of the distance. Councillor Hiscock put the case for the club room and Councillor Ranger, an Enmore Green resident, spoke against. When the vote was taken not surprisingly a large majority voted against because the Enmore Green voters had turned up in strength to the meeting. Councillor Ranger then thanked the voters for their support. This proved too much for the defeated councillor who shouted 'Shut your mouth' and sang the National Anthem at the top of his voice, completely drowning his opponent. It was then that 'personalities were indulged in' as the press reporter euphemistically put it. In other words the two councillors came to blows. Efforts to stop the fracas failed but eventually Arthur left the room and the meeting was closed. Naturally Motcombe's pugnacious councillor was in the news again but in this instance, the publicity must have been unwelcome.

The move to Stourpaine marked the beginning of the decline of Arthur's prowess in the showyard. Other younger competitors were now in the ascendancy; although he continued to exhibit on a more modest scale and win prizes. By the end of the 1920s his name no longer appears among the exhibitors. He was now over seventy years old and had retired with an outstanding record of over three thousand first prizes, numerous cups and other trophies.

In 1931, at the age of seventy-three, the veteran farmer and stockbreeder gave up his Stourpaine Farm and made his final move to his farm at Child Okeford where his eldest son, Victor, had been tenant. Here he continued farming and attending agricultural shows and markets. He was present at a meeting of the Royal Counties Agricultural Society at Basingstoke a fortnight before his death, which came quite suddenly at his home.

His funeral at Child Okeford church was attended by nearly three hundred friends and agriculturalists from over a very wide area that came to pay their respects to one who had begun as a humble farmer but through energy, determination and shrewd judgement had become one of the foremost figures in the agricultural world.

How had it come about that nearly sixty years before, a young Dorset farmer had started out on the path which had led him to fame? From whom had he derived the impetus to become an exhibitor in the showyards throughout the country?

There was at Motcombe another celebrated breeder of pedigree Shorthorn cattle and pigs; namely Nathaniel Benjafield of Shorts Green Farm. He was Arthur's senior by eight years and had already made a name for himself through his successes in the showyards before his emulator and future rival came on the scene. Nathaniel too was active in local affairs; a parish and district councillor and a member of the Shaftesbury Board of Guardians. He was a show judge and a member of the local and the prestigious national agricultural societies. Both were

Nathaniel Benjafield

in the same yeomanry troop and the same lodge of Freemasons. Arthur however did not follow Nathaniel in his political and religious affiliations; he was an Anglican, although his family were Primitive Methodists. In politics he described himself as a Tory of the old school whereas Nathaniel was a Wesleyan Methodist and a Gladstonian Liberal. They were quite different too in character: Arthur was a *bon viveur* who enjoyed social occasions, particularly card parties when he and his farmer friends sometimes sat up all night playing for money and drinking whisky. Nathaniel, on the other hand, was more staid and like most Methodists at that time, a supporter of the temperance and total abstinence movements.

Nathaniel had provided the challenge to which Arthur responded. Although rivals, the two were good friends. Nathaniel died in 1913 at the age of sixty two following a long illness which had compelled him to give up his farm. Arthur attended his funeral and sent a wreath with the message 'with deepest regret for the loss of my lamented loyal and loving friend'.

These alliterative words reflect the depth of his feelings towards one who had contributed in no small measure to his own success.

Twenty-three years later, Arthur Hiscock's obituary records the extent of his achievements: 'A man equally at home talking to kings or the humblest in the land, a shrewd brain that built up an international reputation, yet a simple kindly jovial companion'.

The Rev. Father George Yarnall: Rector of St. James's, Shaftesbury 1900–1927

'THEY be nearly Roman Catholic'. This was how St. James' church at Shaftesbury was often described by many of the local inhabitants in the days when the vernacular was still spoken.

How did it come about that this church, in a small rural parish with a population of under a thousand (most of the town of Shaftesbury was in the parish of Holy Trinity with St. Peters), should be the exception when all the other churches for miles around were by tradition Low Church?

This was due to two men. One was the 9th Earl of Shaftesbury (1869-1961) who was patron of the living. He was a High Churchman and succeeded the Viscount Halifax as president of the English Church Union, whose objects were to defend and further the spread of High Church principles in the Church of England. Lord Shaftesbury had accompanied Lord Halifax on a visit to the Holy See with the idea of promoting reunion between the two churches. The Earl was also a prominent public figure both nationally and locally where he was Lord Lieutenant of Dorset; Chairman of the Dorset County Council from 1924 to 1946; and on a more modest level, President of the Society of Dorset Men for the years 1920-1923.

St James's Church, Shaftesbury

The second man was the incumbent, the Rev. George Hunter Yarnall, who was an American by birth. He had been ordained in the United States but on coming to this country had become a naturalised British subject. It was while he was curate at Romsey Abbey that Lord Shaftesbury had first got to know him when attending an evening service there. His Lordship was so impressed by his abilities and his preaching that when the living of St. James's became vacant he offered

Father Yarnall with choir and servers at St. James's

it by telegram to the Rev. Yarnall who accepted it and was inducted to the benefice on 4th July 1900.

The patron, who was not able to be present at the service, sent a message hoping that this service was but a prelude to a long service in the parish. His Lordship's hopes were to be fulfilled for George Yarnall was to be the Rector of St. James's for 27 years resulting in it becoming a stronghold of Anglo-Catholicism boasting a large choir, many altar servers, excellent music and a colourful liturgy. It attracted large congregations from over a wide area, leading it to be called 'the little cathedral under the hill', but that was some way off.

Initially the going must have been hard; however the new priest was a man of great charisma with a kind, generous and genial disposition. This, coupled with the fact that his style of preaching appealed to his congregation, were valuable assets in winning over his flock.

His first task was to build up the choir and with an excellent organist St. James' soon became noted for the high standard of its music. The so called 'Romish practices' were introduced gradually and over a long period. He always gave an explanation as to their meaning and purpose. A report of the patronal festival in 1908, the year that a new organ was installed, reveals that significant progress had been made. There were three celebrations of the Holy Eucharist on St. James' day

(25th July) which was a Saturday and on the following day the Eucharist was sung to Harwood in E flat when the patron and his wife motored over from Wimborne St. Giles house, the seat of the Shaftesbury family, for the service. At the festival evensong there was a procession, on this occasion the Rector wore a gold brocade cope made by the Altar Guild. The anthem was the *Gloria* from Mozart's 12th mass, when a piano re-enforced the organ. In the week there was a firework display. The report ended by saying that this had been the most successful and well kept patronal festival since the rector had been instituted.

The Angelus was first rung during World War One to remind the faithful to pray for the men of the parish who were at the front.

Father Yarnall would inquire of members of his congregation how they felt about the practices he had introduced. When one member, a housewife, was asked, she replied very positively regarding the midday Angelus, adding 'When I do hear he goo I know 'tis time to put the chiddies (potatoes) on', thus demonstrating that it had a practical use as well as a spiritual one.

The year 1916 was significant because following the gift of a thurible the use of incense was begun. A further advance was made two years later when a statue of the Madonna and Child was given to the church by a grateful worshipper. In the parish magazine Father Yarnall explained why the Mother of God should be honoured in this way. About this time the Stations of the Cross were also donated.

The rector's wife died in 1921. She had been a great help to him in the parish, particularly in his early years.

In 1923 a deaconess was appointed, who had had considerable experience in parish work, and proved to be a valuable asset to the rector, whose health was deteriorating. He suffered badly from asthma, which he had been able to contend with, but with increasing age he had felt unable to continue and resigned the living intending to leave on 4th July 1927, the 27th anniversary of his induction. Sadly this was not to be for he died on 24th June at the age of 68.

So ended his ministry at St. James's where he had worked hard and diligently to restore the 'Faith of England taught of old', leaving it on firm foundations for his successors to consolidate and advance.

The present day St. James's describes itself as being more middle of the road in its liturgy although incense is still used and the statue of the Madonna and the Stations of the Cross are still in place. So too is the side altar where the Sacrament is reserved. This was erected in 1929 by the people of St. James's as a lasting memorial to their rector George Hunter Yarnall, who, over his ministry of 27 years, had created 'the little cathedral under the hill'.

Like Father, Like Son

WHEN Harry Albert Hatch died in February 1985, Motcombe lost its oldest inhabitant. Harry was a Motcombe man and was born at Bittles Green farm. Apart from a few years when he worked away, he had lived in the village all his life.

In his way of life, he was one of the Old School and staunchly independent. He lived alone, without 'mod. cons.' and considered an oil lamp, an oil stove and an old fashioned kitchen grate sufficient for his needs. His only luxury was his wireless.

Despite his great age, he possessed all his faculties and until well into his nineties could be seen daily cycling through the village whatever the weather. If the roads were too bad to cycle, then he walked. With his death a link with the old Motcombe was broken for he had a marvellous memory of village people and events in times long past.

Older Motcombe people will remember when he had a small-

33 Bittles Green when Harry Hatch lived there

holding next to the old Post House and will recall him driving his cows along the village street at milking time, never walking but always on his bike. In those days he was a keen gardener and won many prizes for his vegetables in the annual flower show. It is interesting that Harry's father, Albert Hatch, was also in his day, Motcombe oldest resident. The writer remembers him as a frail old man, bent with age who walked with the aid of two sticks. He died in 1943 at the age of 93. Harry's mother, Mary Ann Hatch, whom he resembled in looks, also lived to a good age, dying in 1942 aged 87.

In their old age they were cared for by their daughter Gertie. Harry also lived with them in the cottage in Frog Lane, where he died on 12 February, six days after his 97th birthday.

Sammy and Eliza Smart

Two well-known personalities in Motcombe over sixty years ago were Sammy Smart and his wife Eliza who lived at number 5 Church Walk, where it is believed Sammy was born.

In the days of the Motcombe estate Sammy was employed as a gardener at Motcombe House and in Lady Westminster's time took care of her flower garden. His own garden was well-kept and well-stocked with vegetables. He had another garden by the church wall where he also had a poultry run. At Motcombe flower shows in the 1930s he was a keen exhibitor and took many prizes.

For some years he was gardening instructor at Motcombe School and is remembered as always wearing a dark blue gardener's apron, old fashioned leather gaiters and hobnailed boots. Sammy was also a bell-ringer at Motcombe church for forty-eight years and for many years he was captain until his retirement in 1935. He died in 1945 aged 83.

Eliza was an accomplished needlewoman, noted for her skill at smocking, with patrons from a wide area, including Lady Theodora Guest. For several years before her death in 1952 at the age of ninety she was confined to her bed following an accident. In her pre-accident days, she always wore a white waist-high, starched apron except on Sundays when she wore her Sunday best. Sammy would discard his apron and wear his derby tweed suit and his best Sunday boots.

They had three sons, Fred, who was killed in the First World War, and twin brothers Tom and George.

Sammy and Eliza are remembered with affection by the writer of this article who, as an after-school errand boy, delivered their groceries once a week. There were just a few items including Sammy's tobacco, an ounce of 'Black Beauty' shag. Weather permitting he was generally in his garden and would invariably call out 'Got my baccy?' Eliza had her bed downstairs by the window and was able to see people walking through 'The Drain' as Church Walk was called in those days.

Bumpy Harris the Builder

ARTHUR Harris was a Motcombe carpenter and builder who, between about 1880 and 1905 built several properties in the village. He was always known as 'Bumpy Harris' but how he acquired this curious nickname has not been discovered.

He was described as being a little man and Lady Theodora Guest, for whom he built Guests Farm at North End in about 1883, referred to him as 'the little Motcombe builder'.

Bumpy lived with his wife, Mary, and their two sons, Sydney and Clarence, in the cottage in Motcombe Street now called 'Roslyn Cottage' which it can be assumed was built by him as were the next pair. They replaced two old cottages which were pulled down.

When Motcombe House, now Port Regis School, was rebuilt during 1893 – 1895 the little Motcombe builder was one of those engaged on its construction and he was the principal builder of 'The Grange' which was completed in 1900 as a new home for Charles Prideaux, proprietor of Motcombe factory.

Sydney and Clarence were employed by their father as carpenters. When they got married he provided them with a home by building a pair of houses originally called 'Knapp Villas' at Knapp Hill. The elder son, Sydney, later took up farming and moved to Guests Farm which his father had built. He was succeeded there by his son and then his grandson. The younger son, Clarence, and his family emigrated to Canada where he continued his trade as a carpenter.

Bumpy died in 1917 and was buried in Motcombe churchyard with his wife who had predeceased him in 1912.

Stephen Smith: a Methodist Pioneer

THE most outstanding of the early Methodists in Motcombe was Stephen Smith, a farmer of Little Lodge Farm, now Forest Farm.

He was converted in about 1762 after hearing the celebrated John Haime preach at Shaftesbury. Thereafter he worked tirelessly to advance the Methodist cause. Through his efforts a strong Methodist society was formed in Motcombe and he became the first class leader. It is recorded that he suffered persecution but nevertheless persevered.

His wife, Elizabeth, was a member of the Broadway family, whose imposing table tomb can be seen in Motcombe churchyard.

Methodists remained members of the Church of England during John Wesley's lifetime and Stephen Smith was no exception. At one time he was a churchwarden at Motcombe church.

Stephen was noted too for his generous financial support for the cause. No doubt he was a liberal contributor towards the building of the first chapel at Motcombe, where John Wesley himself once preached and whose 235th anniversary was celebrated in 2009.

Harold Miles: a Motcombe Man

WHEN Harold Miles died in June 1988 at the age of 92, Motcombe lost its oldest inhabitant. Harold was born at No. 81 Knapp, and apart from the First World War, had lived in the village all his life.

He was also the last of an old Motcombe family, and at least four generations of his family before him had been born and lived in the Knapp/North End area. So with his passing another of the old village names has gone.

Harold was also the last of Motcombe's First World War veterans. He enlisted in the Dorsets when under age, and as an infantryman experienced the horrors of trench warfare. He was wounded, and towards the end of the war became a prisoner of war.

After leaving school he began work at C & G Prideaux Ltd at Motcombe Factory. He returned there after the war, where his job as a boiler man earned him the name 'Tinker' Miles.

Harold and his wife Elsie, who predeceased him some eight years before, lived most of their

Harold Miles

Private Miles

married lives at Elm Hill. When they first lived there, they were surrounded by fields and orchards. What changes they had seen!

To those who knew him well, he would speak in the 'wold Darzet way' – doubtless one of the very few left to do so. Sadly, this has died with him. His way of speaking, together with his fine sense of humour, added greatly to the many hilarious stories he loved to tell of happenings long ago at Motcombe factory when Charles Prideaux was the owner.

He belonged very much to the old village when 'Lordy' was at Motcombe House, Meshach Moore the Parish Clerk and blacksmith, Nathaniel Benjafield farmed at Shorts Green Farm and Nehemiah Arnold, although well over eighty, worked at the factory.

With Harold Miles' passing, one of the few remaining links with the Motcombe of those days has been severed.

The Midnight Baker

THERE are still a few people alive today in the Shaftesbury area who can remember Frederick John Foote, aptly called 'the Midnight Baker' on account of the odd and unsociable hours he chose to call on his customers and also his mode of transport, which was a horse-drawn tradesman's van, dark green in colour with a white roof, old fashioned nearly seventy years ago, which was about the time he gave up his business.

Boldly displayed on both sides of the van, in signwritten letters, were his name and trade,

F. FOOTE PASTRYCOOK AND CONFECTIONER

In fact he was neither, because he bought his cakes and pastries for re-sale. Although it is believed that when he first started his rounds after the First World War he did his own baking. He also sold groceries and sausages.

The Midnight Baker's Motcombe round was on Saturdays, which followed his usual pattern, that is, by starting work when most people were thinking of finishing. Therefore it was not until late in the afternoon when he left his home in Haimes Lane, Shaftesbury, always accompanied by his black retriever, Bruce, who ran on well ahead as if to announce his master's approach.

About half an hour later his patient horse would be seen tied to a telegraph pole while his owner chatted to his first customer. His progress was slow as he was a great talker and never in a hurry. 'If thee didn't bide jawing zoo much thee'd get hwome zooner' was not an infrequent remark from some of his more forthright customers,

Blacksmith's house, showing the porch posts where Lad was tethered

most of whom had known 'Old Footey' since he first started. Usually Fred did not bother knocking on doors; he walked straight in calling out the occupants' name as he did so. Great efforts were made to sell his wares. If a lardy cake had been bought why not dough cake as well? And why not try some sausages?

By about 8 o'clock, winter and summer, he had got about half way. This was the blacksmith's house. Here Lad would be tethered to one of the porch posts while Fred and the blacksmith discussed equine matters; for he was a great horse lover and had no time for motorised transport. Having finally wrenched himself away, he called on his other customers in Motcombe's long and straggling main street. Saturday had only an hour to go when Lad trotted past 'The Royal Oak' which would now be closed, but this was of no consequence to Fred who was not a frequenter of public houses, much preferring his pipe which he kept in his jacket pocket.

His last call was at a house in Elm Hill, about a mile and a half from his starting point. It was the home of Harry Russell who lived alone and had got used to his near midnight caller over the years and was probably glad to have someone to chat to even at that late hour. Harry was often disposed to help out by buying the leftovers particularly if they were of a perishable nature.

At one time there had been customers at North End, a hamlet about a mile from Elm Hill but, not surprisingly, he had lost them. To make matters worse he had been known to leave cakes and suchlike in the outdoor privy if the customers had got fed up waiting and had gone to bed.

It would be past midnight when Fred left Harry Russell's. Those who were still awake would hear the steady trot of the horse, thankful to be going home, and the rumble of the van lit by the dim glow of the candles in the two carriage lamps, as the Midnight Baker made his way through the village street before the long lonely drag up the hills to Shaftesbury in all weathers.

In the early years of the Second World War he was compelled to give up his business due to rationing and shortages so there was no longer a midnight baker. Those on whom he had called at an unearthly hour could now go to bed earlier, but he was greatly missed as he was a kind hearted and likeable man which compensated for the unsocial hours he did his rounds.

Fred was heartbroken when he had to part with his long suffering and faithful horse, which went to a farmer in Gillingham. There he was often visited by his former owner, who would throw his arms around Lad's neck and remain in close embrace for ages.

The former self-employed tradesman became an employee of a Shaftesbury grocer but found it very difficult to adapt to normal working hours; nevertheless he did not have many years in that employment as he died in 1947.

A Personal Reminiscence

IN the early days of the war one of the Motcombe lads used to help the Midnight Baker on his rounds, for which he received sixpence or perhaps on occasions a shilling and some bran for his rabbits. This enabled the nocturnal tradesman to return home somewhat earlier because of the danger of enemy aircraft on their way to Bristol or South Wales jettisoning their bombs if intercepted by our aircraft. Also the blackout posed problems.

The lad usually met his employer on the outskirts of the village, but sometimes would leave his bike behind a hedge and walk up to Shaftesbury to have the pleasure of riding down to Motcombe in the van. Although he was never allowed to take the reins, he was however permitted to put the drug shoe (the Dorset word for a drag) on which served as an extra brake, thus making it easier for the horse when

going down the hills. It was quite
exciting to see the sparks flying
as the drug shoe dragged along
the metalled road. On reaching
the village, the youthful assistant
would go ahead to take some
orders, then collect them from
the van and deliver them. Next he
would take a box of various items
strapped to the carrier of his
bicycle to three or four customers

A drag or drug shoe

in the more distant parts of the village 'on spec'. The prices had to be
known and he was instructed to do his best to sell them.

On one well remembered occasion, there was a pound of 'Dorsella'
brand pork sausages, which were made at Motcombe factory, and were
showing signs that they were past their sell by date. Fred was naturally
anxious to get rid of them so the Saturday boy was told to take them
with other items to Harry Russell who, as has already been stated, was
disposed to buy such items. The line of approach was to tell Mr. Russell
that Mr. Foote considered him to be 'one of the best', 'a good chap' and
was sure Harry would help him out by buying these sausages as their
looks were deceptive and that they were really all right. This approach
was taken but sadly did not work. The prospective buyer picked them
up, smelt them and promptly let it be known in no uncertain terms what
'Footey' could do with them. There being no hope of a sale, the salesman

Elm Hill, about 1906

had to return the rejected items to his boss, on the way, passing the factory where the sausages had first seen the light of day.

The ultimate fate of these suspect items is not known, but what is known is that the Midnight Baker's Saturday boy decided there and then that he was not cut out to be a salesman. Little did he know that he would instead, in later years, become a modest chronicler of a way of life now vanishing, if not already gone.

Uriah Maskell

IN his pamphlet on St Mary's Church Motcombe the Rev George Bennet, a former Vicar, gives details of the rebuilding in 1846.

It may be of interest to know a little about the builder who was awarded the contract with the task of completing the new Church within twelve months. His name was Uriah Maskell, a Shaftesbury man by birth and a stonemason by trade.

At the time of the rebuilding he was living at Bittles Green with his wife and daughter in a cottage most likely to be the present 'Garston Cottage'. His wife's maiden name was Anna Pond and she was a member of a Motcombe family of farmers. He married her in St Mary's Church in 1834. Not long after building the Church, Uriah seems to have taken

Cowherd Shute Farm

up farming as the directories show him living at Cowherd Shute Farm.

In 1858, after Lord Westminster had bought the property, the old farm was pulled down and the present one built. It is a matter of conjecture whether Uriah was the builder, but the farm is built of stone, and he was then described as builder and farmer. Whatever the case, the Maskells were the first occupants, and it was there that Uriah died in 1867. He was buried in the churchyard of the church he had built and where he had served as churchwarden between 1858 and 1861.

The Rev. G. Bennet mentions that when the estate was acquired by the Marquess of Westminster a new prosperity came to the area. One could add that this was particularly true for the building and allied trades. Certainly it was so for Uriah, who left over £9,000 – not an insignificant amount in those days, bearing in mind the fact that he did not own the farm or the land.

3
Places in Motcombe

Ferngore: a Forgotten Place Name

THE article on turnpike roads made reference to Green Lane and commented that the name had fallen into disuse and consequently had been largely forgotten. The same can be said of Ferngore, sometimes written as two words, Fern Gore. This is the land on the right hand side of the road from Motcombe to Semley approaching the sharp bend by the county boundary and the junction with the Sedgehill road. The exact area it covers has not been clearly defined.

There was once a small farm here called Fern Gore Farm and two, possibly three, cottages. The farm was pulled down in the 1830s and not rebuilt. The land, some thirty-two acres, was added to North Hayes Farm. Later a similar fate befell the cottages.

This place name dates back for centuries. It is first recorded in the thirteenth century and in 1300 is mentioned in the perambulation of the Royal Forest of Gillingham as it marked one of the borders of the Forest.

Lady Theodora Grosvenor, in her book *Motcombe Past and Present* published in 1867 says that Ferngore is too well known to require explanation. Although this continued to be so for many years after it is certainly not so today.

On a personal note, the writer of this article recalls an occasion over sixty years ago looking out for glow-worms at Ferngore when cycling after dark from Semley station to Motcombe as it was a place where they were to be found.

Now the glow-worms have gone, and Ferngore forgotten.

Larkinglass Farm

L ARKINGLASS Farm has a unique name as it derives from a machine called a 'larkinglass' which was used to entrap larks. It was fitted with mirrors thus attracting the unfortunate birds that were then caught in a net. 'Larking' is defined as the process of catching larks.

This farm came into being in the middle of the seventeenth century although the present house and buildings, except the barn, are of a later date.

Larkinglass Farm in 1925

One of its fields was called 'Larkinglass' and was in existence in 1663 when a survey of the manor lands was taken. This field could have been where the machine was situated.

In those days larks were quite common and were a culinary item.

The Hamlet of North End

U NLIKE Motcombe Village the hamlet of North End is fortunate in that it has remained relatively unchanged for at least the past hundred years. In fact the number of houses has decreased by one over this period.

North End Farm

It has the distinction too of possessing the finest and most probably the oldest building in Motcombe. This is North End Farmhouse which has its origins in Tudor times. The family who occupied it during the Civil War were staunch supporters of the King and there is an inscription to this effect scratched on one of the stone door posts with the date 1644. Being on the losing side they suffered the consequences by having their property sequestrated. The field names belonging to this farm such as Dunwater, Linhayes, Bean Close, Easthayes and Northhayes date back for centuries. Dunwater first appears in the thirteenth century.

By comparison, Guest Farm opposite is a modern building dating from about 1883. It is named after its original owner, Lady Theodora Guest, née Grosvenor, youngest daughter of the second Marquess of Westminster who once owned the Motcombe estate. The old farm which stood on this site was known as The Blue School Farm and belonged to The Lush's Charity who maintained The Blue Coat School at Shaftesbury later to become the Grammar School.

The last farm, Culverhouse, also has its origins in the distant past and was linked to North End Farm. It has been rebuilt and much altered over the years.

These three farms no longer operate as dairy farms which are almost extinct in Motcombe now.

Culverhouse Farm

The last house, close to the junction of North End Lane with Knapp, was formerly a pair and were the farm cottages for Culverhouse. They were built by the Marquess of Westminster as were the two pairs of brick-built ones with the tap house at the other end of this lane.

Palmer's Place and the Whitakers

WHEN Earl Grosvenor purchased Palmer's Place in 1825 he renamed it Motcombe House. It had been the residence of the Whitaker family since 1648 and during that time had undergone extensive alterations. In fact it had been almost entirely rebuilt by the last Whitaker.

This family had their origins in Wiltshire and had been granted a coat of arms in 1560. Henry Whitaker was the first to reside at Palmer's Place. He was a lawyer but gave up his practice in the Temple when he became recorder and M.P for Shaftesbury. On his death in 1696 he was buried in Motcombe church where his memorial can be seen behind the church door. It was reset there after the church was rebuilt.

The Whitakers had their own chapel in the north aisle of the old church where several of the family are buried, including the last, the Rev. William Whitaker, who died in 1816. His hatchment, the only one surviving, is above the church door. He left an estate of about 800 acres comprising seven farms: Paynes Place; Thanes; Higher Grants (now Frog Lane); Lower Grants (Shorts Green); Butts (Bittles Green); Ferngore, no longer in existence and Burltons, which stood on the site of the present Pear Tree House.

Earl Grosvenor, who was created first Marquess of Westminster in 1831, had bought Shaftesbury in 1820 and the Manor of Gillingham in 1821. Pensbury House and eight Motcombe farms belonged to the Manor: White House; Woodsend (Manor); Little Lodge (Forest); Coppleridge; Dunedge Lodge; Wolfridge; Larkinglass and Woodwater.

So Palmer's Place had now become the Dorset seat of a nobleman, who perhaps considered Motcombe House to be a more appropriate name for a residence of a person of his social rank.

Motcombe House was considerably enlarged by the second Marquess (he had thirteen children) but was pulled down in 1895 when the present mansion, now Port Regis School, was completed.

Old Motcombe House, pulled down when the present Motcombe House was built, now Port Regis School

The Hamlet of Sherborne Causeway

S HERBORNE Causeway is the sixteen-mile stretch of the A30 between Shaftesbury and Sherborne. The A30 was the main highway between London and Lands End and has been in existence since very early times. This causeway was particularly important in mediaeval times when both these towns had markets and abbeys, so much so that an Act of Parliament required that it be kept in good repair; the cost had to be borne by the parishes through which it ran, no doubt provoking much resentment.

Between 1752 and 1865 it was a turnpike road belonging to the Shaftesbury and Sherborne Trust. There was a tollgate at the junction with Lox Lane called Locks Gate. Lox Lane is in the parish of Gillingham and the A30 marks the boundary between Motcombe and Gillingham for a short distance to the left and right of this junction. Shortly after passing what used to be Arnold's filling station, in the Shaftesbury direction, we are in Motcombe and continue to be so for over a mile. Therefore all the houses that straddle this route are in the civil parish of Motcombe and could well be described as the hamlet of Sherborne Causeway.

The five dairy farms that were once here have now been reduced to one, Causeway Farm. There is no pub nor does it appear that there ever has been.

A Lifeboat Mission hall built in 1889 was the place of worship but it no longer exists, nor does the little post office. Long gone too are Gaunt's Causeway Café and Garage and the refreshment rooms where the old post office used to be. Now there is a licensed restaurant. The Blackmore Vale Garage has replaced Arnold's. Here customers are still served with their fuel requirements as in the good old days.

Children from this hamlet usually came to Motcombe School and probably still do. Nadine Abbot, who lived at Causeway Farm, was a pupil when Miss Storey was head teacher and Mrs Belbin was also a teacher. Nadine Abbot is now Lady Cobham and is owner of the racehorse 'Motcombe'.

On Saturday 30 October 1507 a grand procession passed through this part of Motcombe. It was Catherine of Aragon with her retinue en route to London to marry Prince Arthur, Henry VIII's elder brother. She had landed at Plymouth and was making her way by easy stages to her final destination, staying at Shaftesbury Abbey for two nights. After Prince Arthur's death she married Henry VIII and the rest is too well known to repeat here. This information is from the late John Ash's book *West Stour in Dorset*.

Three Farm Names and a Field

AVENUE Farm has now reverted to its former name of Frog Lane Farm. Before this it was called Higher Grants Farm and Shorts Green Farm was Lower Grants as both were the property of James Grant, a partner in the firm of Truman Hanbury and Buxton, brewers of Spitalfields, London. His Motcombe home was a large house called

Frog Lane Farm

Thornhills which stood close to the present Frog Lane Farm. It was pulled down in about 1804 and the stones were used to build what is now the old workhouse, numbers 18-21 Bittles Green.

James Grant died in 1789 and was buried in Motcombe church in the same grave as Richard Ewin from whom he had inherited the two farms. There is a floor slab in their memory in the south aisle.

Grant's name, however, still continues in a wood called Grants Copse near Frog Lane Farm where once bluebells and primroses grew in abundance.

Thaines Farm, (now spelt Thanes) on the other hand, has kept its original name despite the fact that the last Thaine died in 1793. This was Joan, widow of John Thaine. Unlike the farmhouse that dates from the eighteenth century, their home, which was near the farm, has not survived. They too are all buried in Motcombe church and their memorial floor slab is next to Grant's and Ewin's.

One of the fields belonging to Frog Lane Farm is called Turks. At one time it was probably the best known field name in Motcombe mainly on account of the footpath which, in the days when much more walking was done, provided a shortcut between Shorts Green Lane at Little Thatch and the Street by Hayes Mead. Although the footpath is still in use, it is a sign of the times that few people now know the name of the field.

The Hamlet of Coppleridge

THE present spelling of Coppleridge has evolved from an Old English word meaning the ridge at the pollarded oak tree. Some examples of earlier spellings are Copidockridge, Copulridge, Coppedok and Coplery Ridge.

It was once known as the hamlet of Coppleridge and is referred to as such in the 1925 sale catalogue of the Motcombe estate. The area it covers and its boundaries cannot be exactly defined but a document dated 1800 names two fields on the right hand side going down Corner Lane called Great Russells and Little Russells as part of Coppleridge. Proceeding in a westerly direction it included the area around Elm Hill. The hill itself was shown as being in Coppleridge and continued past the two former farms of East and West Coppleridge to end somewhere in the vicinity of Coppleridge Hill.

The dictionary states that a ridge is a long narrow raised land formation with sloping sides. Coppleridge certainly fulfils this criterion.

At one time Motcombe Street ended near the Royal Oak, the present road was only a track so Coppleridge was then quite isolated.

Of the two farms mentioned West Coppleridge, now the Coppleridge Inn, was one of the farms that came into being after the disafforestation of Gillingham Forest in the 17th century and were known as the Manor Farms. When the Marquess of Westminster bought the Gillingham Manor in 1821 considerable improvements were made to them. This was repeated when his son inherited the Manor in 1845. In the case of West Coppleridge, the farmhouse was enlarged and the thatch which covered both farmhouse and the farm buildings was replaced by slates. East Coppleridge Farm, now a private residence, was formerly an alehouse but it had become a farm of about 45 acres when Lord Westminster bought it in 1847.

Turnpike Road and Turnpike Roads

TURNPIKE Road, Motcombe, was originally called Allotment Lane but it extended only as far as the turning leading to Forest Farm near The Kennels. Here it met the old highway which ran from the sharp corner at Coppleridge and after the junction with Allotment Lane continued through what is now Motcombe Park to join the Shaftesbury to Wincanton road (the B3081) west of the entrance to Port Regis School. There was a tollgate here as the B3081 was a turnpike road.

When Earl Grosvenor came to live at Motcombe House he did not like having a road running through his grounds so he had it stopped and the present road built. The tollgate was moved to the junction with the B3081 where the stone built turnpike house still stands.

It was built in 1838 to coincide with the opening of the new road. The date 1866 on the present house is misleading. This is the date when the turnpike road ceased and the house was raised one storey and converted into a pair of farm cottages.

The road from Coppleridge corner to the Forest Farm entrance became a drove road and later a footpath, which it still is. It used to be called Green Lane but this has fallen into disuse and consequently largely forgotten.

A footpath leading from the Forest Farm turning through the fields to the B3081 at Waterloo Farm was also stopped at the same time as the old highway. The road from Shaftesbury to Mere through Motcombe was also a turnpike road. The tollgate was situated at the turning for Motcombe above Pensbury House by Dark Lane.

The A30, which runs through the parish at Sherborne Causeway, was an important turnpike road being the coach road from London to Exeter. The tollgate was at Lock's Lane.

Of the three turnpike houses only one remains and regrettably there is no trace of the other two.

Venues before the Memorial Hall was Built

THERE was no official village hall in Motcombe before the present one was built in 1928. Prior to that, various places were used.

In the first part of the 19th century there were very few secular organisations, however the Motcombe Friendly Society was in existence and had a clubroom opposite the Old Post House. The school, built in 1839, was the meeting place for a bible reading group and later for the night school which began in 1859.

An additional school building in 1874 provided an excellent venue for organisations now coming into being. Here concerts, magic lantern shows, political meetings and, from 1894, parish council meetings took place. But the Band of Hope and the Total Abstinence Society met in the schoolroom of the Wesleyan Methodist Chapel rebuilt in 1870. Coincidentally 'The Royal Oak' was also rebuilt at this time where, on occasions, the Friendly Society held their annual feast. It was the obvious venue too for the annual share out of the Acorn Slate Club, established in 1893.

In about 1918, a scout hut was built for the Motcombe troop, situated between the Old Post House and the Memorial Hall. It acted too as a village hall, dances, whist drives and concerts etc. were regularly held here until the Memorial Hall was officially opened in June 1928.

The Marchioness of Westminster's School Motcombe, 1839–1891, now Motcombe Church of England Voluntary Aided Primary School

A NEW era in Motcombe's history began in the early 1830s when the Earl and Countess Grosvenor came to live at Motcombe House which had been given to the Earl, together with the Motcombe estate, by his father, the first Marquess of Westminster.

The Earl then set about making many improvements to the estate and also adding to it, which, over the course of the next forty years, resulted in Motcombe being extensively rebuilt.

The Countess was particularly interested in the education of the village children. In 1834 she started a new Sunday school and disbanded the old one. Sunday schools in those days taught reading and writing as well as giving religious instruction. The school began with twenty pupils but this number soon increased. It was held in the home of Robert Lilley, who was the master, commencing at 8.30 am and meeting again in the afternoon.

Lady Grosvenor made regular visits accompanied on occasions by her husband, and it is likely that they both assisted with the teaching. Her great ambition however was to establish a day school in a proper school building where the children would be taught by trained teachers. She moved a step closer to achieving her aim at the end of 1838 when she went to the Sunday school to announce that it was soon to end and that a new day school was to begin on the seventh of January next with a new schoolmistress, twenty-one year old Miss Charlotte Perry, who was coming from London with her eighteen year old sister, Mary, as an assistant. Charlotte had been trained at the National Society's school at Westminster. The National Society for the Education of the Poor in the Principles of the Established Church was founded in 1811 and Motcombe's new school, although it would be entirely supported by the

Grosvenors, was to be run on the National Society's principles, that is, as a Church of England school.

Lady Grosvenor's excitement about her school is shown in a letter she wrote to a friend about that time: 'Only imagine we are going to begin a real one (school) at Motcombe and I have got a real live mistress engaged from the National School at Westminster and I want to prevent her finding out, if I possibly can, that I know nothing of any rudiments at all'.

Although the Countess had got her real live schoolmistress she had not got her real school building which was only in the planning stage.

A nearby cottage had been converted to serve as a school temporarily. Nor had the adjoining schoolhouse been built so Charlotte and her sister had lodgings at a farmhouse about a half a mile away.

Lady Grosvenor gave much of her time and attention to helping her real live schoolmistress when the school first opened. Sadly, not long after, she was dealt two shattering blows. One of her daughters, Evelyn, was taken ill with typhus fever and died at Motcombe House on 25th January 1839 aged twelve. Only three days later, news came that her mother, the Duchess of Sutherland, had died at her London home. But her bereavements did not prevent her from resuming her almost daily visits to her school shortly after.

Motcombe School and School House

No firm date is available to indicate when the new school was fully in operation. The date 1839 appearing with the Grosvenor wheatsheaf above the door suggests that it must have been partly in use in that year although the Miss Perrys were still in their lodgings in January 1840 and Lady Grosvenor was visiting both the old and new schools in the following March.

The cost was in the region of seven hundred pounds and architecturally it is of a high standard having the status of a Grade II Listed Building.

Initially there were some problems mostly involving discipline. Her Ladyship recorded that she went to the school and lectured those who had behaved badly, and also visited their parents to tell them to punish their 'rebellious offspring'. One boy was expelled for stealing dinners from other children. Another offence which brought a visit from her was prolonged absence without a good reason. In such cases the parents were told to send the absentees back to school immediately. This continued to be her practice for many years with expulsion for serious misconduct.

On rare occasions when Miss Perry was ill, the Countess, often accompanied by one of her daughters, went to the school and assisted. After five years as Motcombe's first trained teacher, Charlotte Perry resigned. No records exist to show what happened to her after and how her career progressed but she left behind a well established school with about sixty pupils, thirty boys and an equal number of girls.

On the recommendation of a clergyman known to the Grosvenors a married couple, Mr and Mrs Flinn, were appointed as successors to Miss Perry. They commenced their duties in April 1844 on a combined salary of seventy pounds for the first year and eighty pounds per annum thereafter with the schoolhouse and ten pounds per annum for coal for the schoolroom. In the summer of that year all the school children were invited to Motcombe House where they enjoyed a meal of roast beef and plum pudding. This was to be an annual event which continued throughout their patron's long life.

Later, at Christmas time, boots were given, known as the reward boots, which were made by the village cobbler.

In the following year the Marquess of Westminster died and Earl Grosvenor, being his eldest son, inherited the title and the bulk of his great wealth and estates. Eaton Hall, near Chester, had to be the new Marquess and Marchioness's residence and also Grosvenor House, in London. This meant, to their great regret, that they could spend less time at Motcombe, their favourite home.

The school was now called the Marchioness of Westminster's

school. Although her visits were fewer than before, she was kept well informed of all matters of importance.

Early in 1847, while staying at Motcombe House, she learnt that the Flinns were attending the Wesleyan Methodist Chapel in the village. In consequence they were given notice. The full circumstances that gave rise to this drastic action are not known. Perhaps they had received warnings and had ignored them. At that time the church was being rebuilt and services were held in the school which was next door. There was little ecumenical spirit in those days. Motcombe was undoubtedly a Methodist stronghold with two chapels, each with a Sunday school. This was regarded as a threat to the church and it may be that the Westminsters were persuaded by the clergy to take this step.

Lady Westminster then engaged Mr and Mrs Cuckow to replace the Flinns. They started on a salary of eighty pounds per annum plus the usual ten pounds for coal. During the year 1850 complaints were made by the vicar and others regarding Mr Cuckow's behaviour towards some of the pupils. When confronted with these complaints he gave unsatisfactory replies which led to him being asked to leave.

Motcombe School and Church from a watercolour about 1870

The next decade was covered by two couples: the Whites, who left on their own accord in 1855; they were followed by the Atkins. For reasons unknown Mr Atkins was dismissed in 1859.

Mr and Mrs Arthur Blakiston were then appointed. They were held in high esteem by the Westminster's. Mr Blakiston played the organ at the church and trained the choir. He founded the Motcombe Glee singers who gave recitals that were greatly enjoyed, particularly by the Marquess. This well-liked schoolmaster also taught at the night school that had been started in 1859. When they left at the end of 1868, he was provided with a glowing testimonial by the Marchioness.

A few months after their departure the Marquess died leaving his widow the Dorset estates for her lifetime and Motcombe House as her home. This meant that the dowager Marchioness, as she now was, could devote more time to her school, assisted by her youngest daughter, Theodora, who lived with her.

As the numbers in the school were steadily increasing it was found necessary to add another building near the existing one. This was completed in 1874 at a cost of about £520 and could accommodate eighty pupils. The boys occupied the new building and the girls and infants the old one. Between the departure of the Blakistons and the end of 1874 there were three changes in the teachers: the Johnsons, the Burdens and the Walkers served in succession. The last couple only stayed about two months because Mr Walker was dismissed for drunkenness and incompetence.

The expansion of the school, now referred to as 'the schools', meant that an increase in the teaching staff was necessary and marked the end of the period of husband and wife partnerships. When Mr George Plank was appointed in Mr Walker's stead, as head of the boys' school, his wife did not teach. The other posts were held by Miss Cox, who taught the girls and Miss Dawkins, who taught the infants.

Despite advancing years, the Marchioness continued to take an active interest in her schools. On one occasion when she was passing she heard what she described as 'a tremendous row being made by the little demons' during the dinner break. She went into the school to speak to the teachers 'in reproach for such iniquity'. Soon after she donated some toys so that the children had something to play with which, it appears, produced the desired result.

George Plank died in 1880 after a long illness at the early age of forty-six. His successor was a young man of twenty-seven named Loftus Storey who proved to be an excellent schoolmaster. This is demonstrated in the H.M.I. report of 1881: 'The order and discipline are capital and the results of the examination point to sound and careful teaching throughout the school'. In those days pupils were examined orally every year by an H.M.I. (Her Majesty's Inspector of Schools) and a diocesan inspector for religious instruction. Such reports were naturally very pleasing to the patron.

The logbooks for the girls' and infants' schools are extant from 1880 and the boys' from 1883. They provide valuable information on school life at that time. There is also a written account by a former pupil of her school days between 1878 and 1885:

> The day began with prayers followed by scripture. Then came the three 'R's', reading, writing and arithmetic, but not necessarily in that order. Other subjects taught were history and geography. The boys did drawing and the girls' needlework and knitting. There was also singing and much learning was done by rote. The children were graded into standards; one to seven. On reaching standard six the girls were marched to the boys school to take lessons in standard seven with the master.

The teachers were assisted by monitors; older boys and girls who, if considered suitable, taught the younger ones.

Discipline was strict and the cane was frequently used in the boys school. The former pupil recalled that when it was too wet to go out to play they were marched round the desks and had to sing:

> We will march to our places
> with clean hands and faces
> and say our lessons distinctly
> and if we do not do it
> our teachers will know it
> and then to the corner we will surely go

School holidays were shorter in those days: the summer holiday, called the harvest holiday, was the longest. It took place in August and lasted four weeks. There were no half term breaks.

Absenteeism, particularly amongst the boys, for short periods was accepted as their help was required for seasonal tasks such as haymaking, harvesting, potato planting and picking. The girls, too, were absent mainly for domestic work and at harvest time for gleaning. The few pence earned by the children was a welcome addition to the families' meagre income as most of their fathers were agricultural labourers whose wages were abysmally low.

The logbooks record Lady Westminster's visits. An entry in June 1882 reads: – 'Lady Westminster gave a reading lesson to standard III and said they read very nicely'.

This is the last time she appears to have taken a lesson but she was then in her eighty-fifth year. Thereafter she confined herself to inspecting and commenting on the children's work, as evidenced by an entry in July 1885:- 'Visited by Lady Westminster who was well pleased with the needlework and knitting'. Her last recorded visit was in July 1889 when she was ninety-one. On this occasion she made an entry in the boys' school logbook: – 'Much pleased with the school.' and added her signature. However she continued to be present at the children's annual treat at Motcombe House when she was remembered by one of the school girls present as a little old lady dressed in black who sat in a bath chair, to whom they gave a bouquet of flowers on arrival and three hearty cheers at the end.

The Most Honourable Elizabeth Mary, Marchioness of Westminster, died in 1891 three days after her ninety-fourth birthday. In accordance with her wishes she was buried in Motcombe churchyard and her grave is quite close to her beloved schools.

Her funeral was a spectacular event. About five hundred people took part in the procession and well over three thousand lined the route near the church. Of those filing past the grave, forty were her school children; each deposited a bunch of flowers as a tribute to one who had always shown concern for their welfare.

The estates were inherited by her youngest son, Lord Stalbridge, also the schools after whom they were named, but during his time they were put under the control of the Dorset County council.

Many village schools have been forced to close but the Marchioness of Westminster's school, now Motcombe Church of England Voluntary Aided Primary School, has survived and with steadily increasing numbers continues to thrive. The original buildings are still in use although there have been several alterations and additions. Very few today know its origins or that the initials E.M.W. on the 1874 building stand for Elizabeth Mary Westminster, its founder.

The Lord Stalbridge Schools, Motcombe, 1891–1925; Motcombe Church of England School 1925–1939

AFTER the death of the dowager Marchioness of Westminster in 1891, the Motcombe estate was inherited by her younger son, Lord Stalbridge. The schools which his mother had founded now became his property and consequently he was responsible for their upkeep. Therefore they were renamed 'The Lord Stalbridge Schools'.

The new patron was chairman of the London and North Western Railway Company and had other business commitments in London, which meant that he had less time to attend to his schools. His visits were, on average, about three or four times a year. His usual procedure was to 'test the register', that is to call the names to see whether the teachers entries were correct and to receive explanations to account for the absentees. He then signed the logbook after making an appropriate comment such as 'Called the register. All correct'.

Lady Stalbridge sometimes accompanied her husband but on occasions went alone. In 1892 she announced that she intended giving two prizes to each standard at the end of the school year, one for good attendance and the other for best progress.

Another regular visitor was the vicar who took the scripture lessons at least once a week and helped out with other lessons sometimes coming daily when the need arose. This was before the days of supply teachers.

A tragedy occurred in 1900 with the premature death from pleurisy of Loftus Storey, the head of the boys' school. He had been appointed in Lady Westminster's time and was an excellent teacher earning good reports for the school from the inspectors. He left a widow and four children.

In those days schoolteachers were expected to play an active part in village life outside school hours. Loftus Storey was secretary of the Motcombe Friendly Society and the Bell-ringers Guild. He had also taught in the night school. His successor was William Smith who, with his wife Matilda, came to live in the schoolhouse. Mrs Smith taught for several years in the girls' school. He too earned good reports. 'There seems every prospect of Mr Storey's excellent work being continued by his successor,' were the inspectors' comments in 1901 which proved to be correct.

The Education Act of 1902 made the Local Education Authority responsible for the school and a new system of appointing managers had to be introduced. There were to be six: four foundation managers and two local councillors.

Motcombe School's first management committee consisted of: Lord Stalbridge (chairman), The Hon. Hugh Grosvenor (Lord Stalbridge's son and heir), The Rev. R.E. Tanner (the Vicar), George Allen (Lord Stalbridge's land agent), Arthur Hiscock appointed by the County Council and Nathaniel Benjafield, appointed by the Parish Council. These two were prominent Motcombe farmers. The former was a churchwarden and his children had attended the school. The latter was a staunch Wesleyan Methodist. Motcombe then had a Primitive and

Motcombe School, built 1839

a Wesleyan chapel which many of the school children attended.

The newly constituted committee held their first meeting on Saturday 18 July 1903 in the boys' school. Only three managers were present although enough to be quorate. Not surprisingly Lord Stalbridge was elected chairman and the vicar the correspondent. In accordance with the provisions of the Act the stock and store book, logbook and registers were all examined. Other matters dealt with were the cleaning which was done by three girls at sixpence a week. A woman was paid four shillings a quarter for scrubbing. Lastly it was decided to get an estimate for seven tons of coal and three of coke. These very brief minutes ended with a list of the school holidays which totalled nine weeks.

The last meeting that his Lordship chaired was in April 1905. Shortly afterwards he left the village due to acute financial problems, which compelled him to give up living at Motcombe House, and spend the rest of his days at his London home.

The estate, including the school buildings, remained his property although he had contributed little to their maintenance in recent years. Of concern to the children was that with Lord Stalbridge's departure they were deprived of their annual party at Motcombe House.

Three years later 'the schools'' became 'the school' because it was decided that both boys and girls should be taught together throughout and not segregated when they had passed the infant stage. These changes entailed certain alterations to the buildings. The owner's contribution amounted to £10 out of a total cost of £127. The rest came from donations, grants and a voluntary rate.

Lord Stalbridge died in 1912. Although still a foundation manager he had not attended any meetings since his departure for London in 1905. In fact he had severed all links with the village leaving his agent in charge. His son, who succeeded to the title, was already a foundation manager but had only been present at two meetings since 1903. Attendance by the other managers, except for the vicar, had been poor sometimes consisting of only two and thus not quorate. Nevertheless decisions were made and acted on.

The new Lord Stalbridge did not take up residence at Motcombe House until January 1914 and attended his first managers' meeting in the following May when, as was to be expected, he was elected chairman. The outbreak of the First World War three months later meant that he was recalled to his regiment and was absent throughout the war years.

The passing of various Education Acts, particularly those of 1870 and 1902 saw an increase in officialdom. The first mention of attendance officers occurs in the 1890s when Loftus Storey records that he was given forms to be completed with respect to the names of irregular attendees and absent children. These officials then visited the parents to ascertain the reasons and reminding them that they faced prosecution if their children were persistently absent without good cause. Attendance figures were important because they were the basis for government grants. Hence the reason why the all-important register was completed faithfully with appropriate explanations if any alterations had to be made.

That the school was no longer entirely supported by the first Lord Stalbridge is proved by entries in the logbook recording the receipt of grants for £30 on two occasions and of annual grants for 'wear and tear'.

The school dentist and medical officer and later the head nurse, or 'nit nurse' as she was called by the children, came on the scene. The medical officer had powers to order the school to close in cases of infectious illnesses. A bad outbreak of scarlet fever in 1914 caused its closure for ten weeks.

An example of the increasing power of the educational bureaucracy occurred in 1909 when the managers decided that the afternoon school should begin at 1.30pm instead of 1.45pm. Notice was sent to the Education Officer at Dorchester to this effect but a reply was received that the school must start at 1.45pm as 'sanction for altering the timetable had not been given by them or the inspector'.

The war years brought problems. There was a high turnover of staff although Mr. Smith remained. An attempt to transfer him to another school temporarily was successfully resisted by the managers. The children had time off and extra holidays to pick blackberries to send to a factory to make jam for the troops. They also collected acorns and chestnuts for a munitions factory (to make cordite), although the logbook omits to say that this was their purpose.

The school managers were now visiting the school to test the registers and watch activities, including Lady Stalbridge, who had taken her husband's place as chairman in his absence. Rewards for good attendance had been introduced in the 1890s. They took the form of medals and certificates and were presented to the winners at the end of each school year. It is surprising that despite all the illnesses that afflicted children in those days, one boy achieved an unbroken attendance record of seven years and a girl five years. However both lived within easy walking distance of the school whereas some children had up to three miles to walk.

In 1906 William Smith gave up the schoolhouse and for reasons unknown moved to Shaftesbury, resulting in a daily walk of over two miles each way. This move did not please the managers but nothing could be done, not even by the powerful Lord Stalbridge who, after his return from the war, resumed his position as chairman of the managers. He expressed his concern to the education authorities that if the schoolmaster did not live in the schoolhouse then the discipline of the boys in the village would suffer as a consequence.

It seems that the school authorities exercised control over the children when out of school as well. In 1911 two children were brought before the managers and 'urged to improve their conduct out of school hours'. Punishment of pupils in those days for a variety of offences, including sulking and displays of temper, was usually accepted and supported by the parents. It is known that some parents would punish their offspring again for misbehaving but the records reveal instances where they disagreed and showed this by keeping the offender away from school for periods ranging from half a day to two or three days. This happened both in Loftus Storey's and William Smith's time. The latter had to contend with an angry parent who came to the schoolhouse and 'used filthy language and assuming a fighting attitude threatened great things'. Oddly, on one occasion, Loftus Storey records that a boy had refused to stay behind after school with the others to help tidy up, stating that he did not come to school to clean up afterwards. He appears not to have been punished. At another time a complaint was received that some boys had stolen gooseberries from a garden on their way to school. The constable was called to the school and the culprits' names taken. It appears that the matter was not pursued. In those days the fact that the 'bobby' was after them would have struck terror in their hearts.

Some Motcombe School 'scholars', about 1919

The early years of the 1920s proved to be a difficult time mainly due to staffing problems and various illnesses which affected both teachers and pupils. In 1920 the school was closed for five weeks following an outbreak of measles and three weeks in 1925 on account of diphtheria. The inspectors report of 1921 reflects these problems, referring to the cramped conditions, there were about one hundred pupils at this time, and the disadvantages resulting from frequent changes of staff. To add to these difficulties in 1925 Lord Stalbridge decided to sell the Motcombe estate, including the school, which caused the managers great anxiety as well as the parochial church council because it was a national or church school. The vicar, on behalf of both bodies, wrote to his Lordship begging him to exclude the school from the sale and give them the opportunity of purchasing it by private treaty. There was great joy and relief when a reply was received stating that he would convey the school to the church as a gift. So it now became known as Motcombe Church of England School.

In the following year William Smith, having reached the pensionable age of sixty, tendered his resignation. On 30 July 1926 he made his final entry in the logbook, 'After 26 years service in this school I, today, terminate my engagement as Head Teacher'.

Miss Beatrice Cribb was appointed to succeed him at a salary of £270 per annum less £20 per annum for the rent of the schoolhouse. She introduced some new ideas, one of which was to involve the parents more in the life and work of the school. An open afternoon for parents and friends was first started in December 1926 when the children's work was on display and they entertained their visitors with songs, dances and recitations. Miss Cribb commented that 'It was a pleasure to meet so many mothers and to see their keen interest in the work'. Another innovation was the instalment of a wireless for the children to listen to broadcast lessons. These were used on a regular basis. A percussion band was also started in which the children showed a keen interest.

The excellence of Miss Cribb's work was reflected in the H.M. Inspector's report in 1933 when the school was graded as class I, that is, a school deserving special commendation. This announcement was naturally received with great pride and gratification by the staff and managers.

The vicar at that time was the Rev. David Watkins-Jones. He too proved to be of great benefit to the school. He was conscientious, hardworking and businesslike. The minutes of the managers' meetings which he, as chairman and correspondent wrote, reported the proceedings in detail and financial statements appeared for the first time.

After eight years as head teacher Miss Cribb resigned, giving as her reason her state of health and that in consequence the work was proving too much for her. She expressed her view that the task was more suited for a man. Obviously the managers did not concur as they appointed another woman, Miss Frieda Storey, who commenced her duties on 3 September 1934 occupying the schoolhouse with her sister. At that time there were sixty-five pupils and two other teachers.

The school was again placed in class I in 1936 thus showing that Miss Storey had maintained the standard set by her predecessor. The diocesan inspectors' reports on religious education were very laudatory in both these teachers' times. The curriculum was also expanding. The senior boys had to go to Shaftesbury once a week for carpentry lessons and the senior girls for cooking.

It had been known for some years that a new school was to be built at Shaftesbury for children between the ages of eleven and fourteen. Only those who had 'passed the scholarship', on average about two a year, had left Motcombe school at eleven to go either to the Grammar School for boys or the High School for girls at Shaftesbury or to the mixed Gillingham Grammar School. The senior school, as it was called, opened on 9 January 1939 and the senior Motcombe school children were bussed there daily to be educated with their contemporaries from the surrounding area. Motcombe School was demoted to a junior school with forty pupils on the register and began a new phase in its history. Coincidentally that year was its centenary but there were no celebrations. War clouds were gathering and the pupils were being acquainted with air raid procedures while the teachers were attending A.R.P. (Air Raid Precautions) lectures.

Naturally there had been many changes since Lady Westminster had first started her school. The use of the cane, which had been the language of communication between teacher and pupil in Victorian and Edwardian times, had dropped substantially but it was still a method of punishment for more serious offences and for persistent offenders. For boys two strokes on the hand was the norm or, very rarely, two 'on the seat'. There are no extant records how the girls fared. Nearly thirty years were to elapse before the Plowden Report would recommend its abolition in primary schools.

There had also been some advances in the governance of the school since Lady Westminster had governed alone. In 1939 the management committee was no longer dominated by the all powerful squire; it consisted of the vicar, three farmers, a tradesman and a woman. Representation of parents and teachers was yet to come, nevertheless things were moving, albeit slowly, in a more democratic direction.

Motcombe Church of England Voluntary Aided Primary School: its History From 1939 to 2006

THE start of the spring term on 9 January 1939 marked the beginning of a new chapter in the history of Motcombe School; for it then became a primary school with a reduced age range of five to eleven. Pupils above that age had to go to the new secondary modern school at Shaftesbury, with the exception of those who had been awarded places at the Grammar School or High School. As a result the number of pupils fell from fifty-six to forty, which led to a reduction in the teaching staff from three to two. The head's position was not in question, therefore the choice lay between Mrs Belbin, the infants' teacher, and Miss Turner, who was responsible for the juniors. Mrs Belbin was the more senior both in age and service so it was decided that Miss Turner should be the one to go. Fortunately she soon secured a new post at a school in Gillingham.

It was a coincidence that 1939 should also be the centenary of the school but there were no celebrations, in fact no mention was made of this event in the log book or in the minutes of the managers' meetings.

The outbreak of the war on 3rd September caused a major upheaval; about fifty evacuee children and two teachers arrived in the village from London, but without any school equipment. Consequently the Motcombe children were obliged to have their lessons in the morning and the evacuees in the afternoon, however this situation only lasted a month as desks arrived for the evacuees allowing the local children to resume their lessons according to the timetable and revert to their usual hours. Since there were two separate buildings the schools could operate independently of each other.

In 1942 the evacuees' school was closed due to a sharp decline in numbers, resulting in the junior children being merged with the Motcombe children and the seniors being transferred to the secondary school at Shaftesbury. The London County Council continued to supply a teacher at Motcombe throughout the war years bringing the number to three.

Despite the many difficulties and problems experienced at that time, the school seems to have coped quite well under the able headship of Miss Storey, who received much support from the vicar, The Rev. David Watkins-Jones, in his capacity as correspondent and chairman of the management committee. His sudden death in 1944 was a great loss to the school and the parish.

The austerity of the war years continued for some considerable time after peace came and education was no exception. Despite this the H.M.I report in 1950 commented that the teaching was well above average and that high standards had been attained in the fundamental subjects.

Mrs Belbin resigned in 1952 having reached retirement age. She was replaced by Mrs Hurley, an experienced teacher, who was in charge of the infants until her death in 1961 within a year of her retirement.

Another retirement took place in 1959: that of Miss Storey after completing twenty-five years as headmistress. She had seen many changes during her time at Motcombe, particularly in the post-war years. The curriculum had widened and officialdom had increased with an assortment of officials, advisers and experts now visiting the school. Frieda Crosby Storey was 'one of the old school' who considered it her duty to play an active role in village life outside school hours. She had

Mrs Carter's infants, 1967

taught in the Sunday school, certainly a busman's holiday; served on the parochial church council and the parish council; organised keep fit classes and others; and was a collector and the treasurer of the Motcombe coal and clothing clubs. She continued to live in the village after her retirement until her death in 1977 at the age of eighty-two.

Mr Stanley Whittaker was her successor. When he took over there were sixty-seven on the role with one permanent teacher and one supply. It was at this time that Mrs Stainer rejoined the staff. She was the former Miss Turner who had had to leave in 1939.She completed sixteen years at Motcombe before retiring in 1976. Stanley Whittaker only stayed for four terms. His replacement was Mr William Hockey. This was his first headship. During his first year there was an inspection by the H.M.I's who were satisfied with the running of the school and congratulated the head on his achievements in such a short time, also remarking on the happy atmosphere in the school. The increased number of pupils was noted, seventy-two, and it was predicted that the number would reach eighty by the end of that school year

One of the new head's innovations was the annual prizegiving ceremony. This proved to be a successful venture and continued to be so for many years. During the exceptionally hard winter of 1962/3, the school, in common with many others, suffered as a result of frozen pipes and the lack of transport, which meant no school dinners. On one occasion recorded in the log book, the headmaster had accompanied some children home due to the treacherous state of the roads.

The former Boys' School at Motcombe built 1874

In the following year plans for the much needed modernisation of the school were approved and put into operation. There was considerable inconvenience to staff and pupils until the alterations were completed but in the end it all proved worthwhile for on 14 December 1964 the Bishop of Sherborne dedicated the new buildings. Mr Hockey, however, did not stay very long after to enjoy the benefits as he resigned at the end of the following year to take up a new post. A relief head took charge for a term until Mr Ivor Hawkins began his duties as head teacher on 19th April 1966.

Realising the value of parent teacher organisations in the life of a school and the supportive role they played particularly in raising much needed funds for school purposes, he drew up a new constitution for Motcombe's P.T.A with the title 'The Motcombe School Association' which was adopted at the next A.G.M.

In the late 1960s considerable time was spent by the school managers and the parochial church council in deliberating whether the school should continue its status as voluntary aided or become a controlled school. It was felt that little would change except that the church, through its representatives on the school management committee, would have less influence in the appointment of future heads and in consequence this could mean that he or she may not be a member of the Church of England or indeed a Christian. Finance was the real cause of their concern; the cost of maintenance was ever increasing and their income decreasing. In the end it was decided to recommend that the existing status should continue.

Another new venture which was introduced at that time was an open day when parents and those interested could visit the school at any time during the day, including assembly and dinner, to see the children at work. This brought an excellent response and became an annual event.

The first school fête was held on 24 September 1966. It was most successful providing much needed funds for 'extras'. Later it was combined with the village fête and the children's contribution usually took the form of dancing displays, exhibitions of their work and various competitions.

At the end of the seventies there was a great deal of discussion and consultation regarding the future of rural schools in the district. Motcombe, it was feared, might have to close because there had been a substantial drop in numbers. This, not surprisingly, brought strong opposition and the school authorities received the backing of local public bodies and influential individuals to help prevent this threat. Happily the battle was won and Motcombe retained its school, but some villages were not so fortunate.

Motcombe First School in 2003

Although the school was saved the schoolhouse was not. The diocesan authorities, who obviously did not consider it to be an integral part of the school, decided to sell it. It had been the head teacher's home since 1839 when the school was built, except for a short period during William Smith's time (1900-1926), when it had been rented out.

As for the school the seventies had been a relatively quiet period. There were alterations to the syllabus for religious education and the close links with the church were maintained. The vicar usually took the assembly once a week. There were more liaisons with the two private schools in the village, Port Regis and The Grange. The former offering excellent facilities for sport, music, art and technology.

The new decade was not to be a repeat of the seventies. The rate of change accelerated rapidly both in the school and in the village. Motcombe had been a close-knit community, most of the inhabitants had lived here all their lives as had generations of their families before them. The numerous dairy farms and the milk and bacon factory had provided employment for the majority but the number of farms was decreasing and the factory was being run down, thus employing fewer staff. Many more homes were being built bringing in people from all parts of the country. So no longer did one know everybody in the village as had been the case. The strangers or outsiders as they were referred to by the locals were becoming the majority. This too had its effect on the school as the newcomers who were parents and had children of school age were often more vocal in making suggestions, criticising and putting forward new ideas. The schoolteachers had by now detached themselves from the life of the village and in some instances lived a considerable distance away.

In 1980 school managers were renamed school governors probably in preparation for the wider powers and increased responsibilities they would be granted in a few years time.

Mr Hawkins relinquished his duties in 1981 after fifteen years and one term at the school as he had now reached retirement age. Mrs Judith Hall, who lived at Wimborne, was appointed relief head and continued in that capacity until the end of the school year in 1983. On 1st September of that year Motcombe school commenced another chapter in its history. Due to the re-organisation of education in the Shaftesbury area into a three tier system it became a first school for those between the ages of five and nine. A new middle school had been built at Shaftesbury for the nine to thirteen year olds.

This coincided with the appointment of a new head at Motcombe, Mrs Felicity Stebbings, but her headship was brief: she was granted maternity leave in December 1985 at the end of which she decided not to return and tendered her resignation. Mrs Hall came back to cover her absence and for the period before Mr Roger Withey took over in September 1987. There were then forty on the roll, two other teachers and fourteen governors, the numbers having been increased. There was now a governor for every three children. The eighties ended with the sesquicentenary of the school. Although there had been no celebrations to commemorate the centenary in 1939 things were very different in 1989. The whole school attended a church service on 8 June when old pupils were also invited. After the service a large party was held when a representative from the diocese was present. There was also a private party held in the village hall arranged for those who had attended the school during the First World War period and the early 1920s.

For the teachers, inset days started in the mid-eighties. Inset is an acronym for in-services education and training and it became a statutory condition of employment. This meant days off for the teachers to train and days off for the pupils.

It was during this decade that computers came on the scene. The first arrived in 1984 and the second some time after, which allowed one for each classroom.

Another introduction was a playgroup for the pre-school age children. They occupied one of the school buildings for several years until they moved to new premises in the school grounds in 1994.

The education act of 1988 provided for a national curriculum in state schools. This of course initially involved much time in preparatory meetings at various venues in a variety of places. Meetings and going to meetings feature prominently in the education world of today.

Mr Withey tendered his resignation in 1994 having been appointed head of West Moors First School. Mrs Kate Lewis-Evans, member of the teaching staff, took over as acting head and was later made permanent head. The numbers had started to increase again and an additional class had to be created.

It was during the 1990s that Ofsted (the Office for Standards in Education) took over the responsibility for inspection from the H.M.Is. Motcombe School was first inspected by this body in 1996 and again in 2000. At both times the results were very positive.

This was a period when the school enjoyed many successes particularly in music and sporting competitions. The links with Port Regis School were maintained but the Grange school had closed.

Mrs Lewis-Evans, who lived in the village, retired in 2002 having served as head for seven years, the same as her predecessor

The new head, Mr Andrew Walker, only stayed for two years. There was a temporary appointment until Mrs Ann-Marie Kampf became head teacher in January 2005. In the meantime, the school, after twenty years as a first school, reverted to its former status as a primary school with effect from September 2004. Again this was on account of the Shaftesbury area adopting a two tier system.

Confident of its future an extension has been built consisting of new classrooms and a fine hall which was dedicated by the Bishop of Sherborne at a service held on 5th May 2006 when the children played an active part.

At the end of the school year in July 2006 there were eighty-nine on the role. With more housing development planned in a few years time the figure should well exceed the hundred mark.

Doubtless, the Marchioness of Westminster, whose grave is only a few yards away, would be delighted that her school, which she founded nearly one hundred and seventy-three years ago, is still in operation and that the exterior of both buildings and the playground remain mostly unchanged. She would be pleased to see the children in their uniforms looking much healthier, better fed and better clothed than they were in her day. She would have noted too that the teachers are more professional and that the relationship between them and their pupils has radically changed, particularly with regard to discipline. She would be amazed at the amount of paperwork they have to contend with and would recall the times when she had been the sole administrator.

Nevertheless her comment in the log book in 1889,'much pleased with the school' would, if written now, be the same.

All over the country in the past few decades village schools, despite petitions and protests, have been forced to close. Several schools in the area have suffered this fate and Motcombe was once threatened but the axe did not fall. There is every reason to be optimistic about its future in view of the recent expansion of the village.

The Memorial Hall

THERE was no village hall in Motcombe until the present one was opened in 1928.

It had been acknowledged before the First World War that a place for social gatherings was needed so, when the first Baron Stalbridge died in 1912, the idea was conceived that a village hall dedicated to his memory would be a fitting tribute to him; for Lord Stalbridge had been a good landlord, and had been held in high esteem by his many tenants. One of these was Charles Prideaux, proprietor, of Motcombe, Shaftesbury. It was mainly his efforts and sound business acumen that eventually brought the idea to fruition.

The war and the need to raise sufficient funds were the chief reasons for the gap of sixteen years. Generous financial help was received from members of the Grosvenor family and others. The second Lord Stalbridge donated the land. But the wait was worthwhile; for Motcombe can boast a fine village hall and the recent renovations should ensure the memorial to Richard de Aquila Grosvenor, First Baron Stalbridge will be in use for many years to come.

The Memorial Hall, Motcombe

There is also another memorial to Lord Stalbridge in Motcombe – a stained glass window in the church. He also had a railway locomotive named after him, 'Lord Stalbridge', in the George the Fifth class, built at Crewe in 1913 and a dock, the Stalbridge Dock, at Garston on Merseyside.

Motcombe Field Names

FIELD names generally have fallen into disuse mainly due to the decline in agriculture. Motcombe is no exception, although there are at least three farms where the owners call their fields by their original names, which in some cases are several centuries old.

Probably the best known field name was 'Turks' on account of the much used footpath through it linking Shorts Green Lane with The Street. It is smaller than its original size due to some of the land bordering Shorts Green Lane being bought by Charles Prideaux to build homes for the workers at his factory. The adjacent field is 'Northayes', it too lost a few acres to provide land for the recreation ground, the hall and the war memorial.

Motcombe folk in past times certainly knew and used the field names near their homes. 'Corner Acre' for example is behind the garden nursery and neighbouring properties in The Street. Adjoining 'Corner Acre' to the south is 'Blackhouse' where there is a brook which, on occasions, used to flood, when one heard it said that the water was out over 'Blackhouse'.

At the rear of the bungalows in Bittles Green is 'Lakehouse Mead' a former allotment site. Another site was 'Bowers' which was on the left hand side going up the hollow. The correct name is 'Puckmore Hollow' taking this name from a field on the right hand side at the top. A third site was 'Brickells Plot' now part of 'Willow Way'.

Some names were lost when fields were combined. 'Burts' and 'Bowling Alley' (there was a bowling alley here in the seventeenth century) with others in this area are examples. They were behind the school and churchyard.

Before the present recreation ground came into being in the 1920s, a field called 'Hayes Mead' at the rear of the old workhouse was used for recreational activities and fêtes. This became known as 'The Cricket Field' and continued to be so called long after the present recreation ground took its place.

Some years ago a group of Motcombe villagers had the forethought to make a map showing the field names. Much work and research was put into producing this. It is in the form of a triptych and can be seen in the hall on the east wall.

Three Lakes, a Brook and a River

A LAKE is defined as a large expanse of water entirely surrounded by land. There is however another meaning, now obsolete, which is a small stream or water channel.

Three of the several streams in Motcombe once had names and were called lakes but over the course of time they have been forgotten. They are Cramburne Lake, Jay's Lake and Cusborne Lake.

Cramburne Lake is the stream that crosses under the bridge at Bittles Green, continues behind the houses towards the church, then through Church Walk and runs parallel with the road at the lower end of the village until it veers sharply to the left near a cottage.

Shorts Green Farm provides the first glimpse of Jay's Lake where it runs through the garden and passes under the bridge by the 'Royal Oak'.

Cusborne Lake is on the outskirts of the village. It runs under the Semley road near Knapp and can be seen again at the bridge at the bottom of Coppleridge Hill.

The brook is the Fernbrook, visible from the bridge on the Gillingham road near Lox Lane. Although small, it has an important function as it forms the boundary between Motcombe and Gillingham.

Travelling along the Mere road, a view can be had of the river, the Lodden, by Lawn Bridge. It too marks the boundary between the two parishes at the northern end.

The lakes and the brook link up with the river, which joins the Stour, Dorset's principal river, below Gillingham.

The Sale of the Motcombe Estate

THE year 1925 is an important date in Motcombe's history because it was the year when the estate was sold.

Lord Stalbridge (the second Baron Stalbridge) had already disposed of his Shaftesbury and Stalbridge estates and it was thought that he would keep Motcombe and continue to live at Motcombe House, but his lordship decided to sell up and leave despite the fact that some members of the family, including his wife and son, were not happy with the idea and tried to dissuade him. It also led to the resignation of two of the trustees, friends of his father, the first Baron Stalbridge.

All the tenants were given the opportunity to purchase their properties prior to the sale and several did so.

The sale by auction consisting of 165 lots and including properties in Gillingham and Shaftesbury was to take place on 27th July but it was bought beforehand by two property speculators Messrs.Gaskain and Benton. They also purchased the water supply. Tenants could however continue to buy their properties.

In 1929, there was a further sale by auction of 97 lots, the vendors now being Gaskain and Benton. This time Motcombe House and the grounds were included but it was not sold and was threatened with demolition. However Charles Prideaux, the proprietor of Motcombe factory, stepped in and made an offer of £10,000 which was accepted. The new owner never lived there and it remained empty for ten years, except for a caretaker.

There was a final sale of the remaining portions comprising 37 lots in 1933 which were mainly properties that had not been sold in 1929 including four Motcombe farms.

With the sale of the estate and Lord Stalbridge's departure Motcombe now entered a new phase of its history with Charles Prideaux as the principal property owner and most prominent person in the village and his firm, C & G Prideaux Ltd., the chief employer.

Motcombe in 1800

TWO hundred years ago Motcombe formed part of the manor of Gillingham and Sir Francis Sykes was the Lord of the Manor. He did not reside here as the family seat was at Basildon in Berkshire.

William Whitaker was the local squire. He lived at Palmers Place, the name of the old Motcombe House, which had been the family home since 1648.

At that time the church had the status of a chapel with a curate in charge, because Motcombe was in the large ecclesiastical parish of Gillingham.

The Methodists had a meeting house in the village on the same site as the present chapel.

The 'Bull Inn' was the principal hostelry: it was situated in The Street next to 'Brookside'. There were also some beerhouses including the 'Royal Oak', not however the existing one which was built in 1870 as a hotel.

According to the 1801 census, the population of Motcombe, which included Enmore Green and Sherborne Causeway, was 917.

The area around the church, the lower end of The Street and Bittles Green contained most of the dwellings.

Fortunately, despite all the changes, quite a number of the farms and houses which were in existence in 1800 are still surviving today.

Motcombe in 1900

ONE hundred years ago the first Baron Stalbridge was the Lord of the Manor. He resided at his newly built mansion, Motcombe House, which is now Port Regis School.

It was the time of the Boer War and two of his sons were on active service in South Africa as well as several men from the village.

A tragedy occurred at the school, Loftus Storey, the schoolmaster, died aged forty-one leaving a wife and four children. He was succeeded by William Smith.

At the church, there was a new vicar, the Rev. R. Tanner and a new organist, Mr. W. Hallett. The Wesleyan and Primitive Methodist Chapels were thriving. Both, giving enthusiastic support to the Motcombe branch of the Band of Hope and Total Abstinence Society.

Business at the dairy and bacon factories continued to expand and Charles Prideaux, the proprietor, moved into his new home, The Grange, now retirement homes.

This was the year when Motcombe Cricket Club was formed. There was no recreation ground then, matches were played in a field behind the old workhouse (18–21 Bittles Green), known as the cricket field, where there was a pavilion.

The two big events of the year were the annual fête of the Motcombe Friendly Society, held at Whitsuntide, and the Bonfire Carnival, which took place on Saturday 9 November, when decorated horse-drawn floats paraded through the village headed by Gillingham Town Band. Motcombe's fife and drum band was also in attendance.

In September the village school children had their annual party at Motcombe House given by Lord and Lady Stalbridge. At that time the school was mainly supported by his Lordship.

Also in that month, the Stalbridges' first grandchild, Patrick Ivor Hugh, son of Aubrey Smith and the Hon. Elsie Smith née Grosvenor, was christened in Motcombe Church.

Arthur Hiscock of Manor Farm and Nathaniel Benjafield of Shorts Green Farm continued their numerous successes at agricultural shows up and down the country with their pedigree cattle and pigs. Both men and Arthur Hiscock in particular, made Motcombe internationally famous as a centre for breeding these prize winning animals which were exported to all parts of the world.

In 1900, a Shorthorn bull bred by Arthur Hiscock was sold for 200 guineas and shipped to Buenos Aires.

Even in those days Motcombe had its traffic problems, complaints were made about the furious rate at which the milk carts were being driven through the village after dark without lights and to be really safe, according to the complainant, one would have to get into the ditch when they went by.

Motcombe in 1905

THE year 1905 was not a good one for Motcombe as it was marred by the departure of Lord and Lady Stalbridge from their home at Motcombe House, which was then a newly built mansion, to live permanently at their much smaller London house in Sussex Square.

Lord Stalbridge was in dire financial straits and had he not taken this drastic action he would have been made bankrupt; but in doing so he saved the Motcombe estate, which enabled him to pass it on to his eldest son on his demise. It was a big sacrifice to make as his income now came mainly from his remuneration as chairman of the London and North-Western Railway.

Motcombe too was adversely affected. Apart from the job losses among the estate employees, the school, which had been mainly supported by his Lordship, had to be put under the control of the Dorset County Council and the children were deprived of their annual party at Motcombe House. The Church and other institutions as well as the tradesmen also suffered financially.

However the impoverished peer did give permission for a bazaar and fête to be held at Motcombe House on 7th and 8th June of that fateful year to raise money for a new organ in the Church, but the former occupants did not return for this event nor were they present on any future occasions except after their deaths.

When Lady Stalbridge died in 1911 she was brought back to Motcombe to be buried in the churchyard and was followed by her husband a year later.

Motcombe in 1907

THE only notable event in Motcombe in 1907 was the dedication of a new organ, choir stalls and pulpit in the church. The ceremony was performed by the Bishop of Salisbury on 24th September, but, although this was on a Tuesday it was nevertheless well attended.

The old organ had been situated at the west end of the church so, too, were the choir, but the new organ was installed in the chancel, also the new choir stalls. There they remained for seventy years when the organ was moved to where its predecessor had been and the choir stalls were also moved leaving a bare chancel. The pulpit alone remains in its original position.

Motcombe Church outing to Gough's Caves, Cheddar, about 1922

The choir in 1907 consisted of girls, boys and men but were not surpliced. The vicar was the Rev. George Bradley-Jones. The first Baron Stalbridge, who was the younger brother of the first Duke of Westminster, owned the Motcombe estate.

In addition to the church there were two chapels, a Wesleyan Methodist and a Primitive Methodist, the latter is now a private residence called 'Brookside'.

There were well over a hundred pupils at the school. William Smith was the head; his wife also taught there together with another teacher.

Charles Prideaux's factory was continuing to expand with depots at Stalbridge, Shillingstone, Evercreech and Mere.

'The Royal Oak' belonged to the Motcombe estate and was let to the Dorset Public House Trust. The manager was William Harber.

Apart from about twenty-five farms and smallholdings there were two blacksmiths, one wheelwright, two builders, one of whom was an undertaker, four grocers, one baker, one shoemaker and repairer, one basket maker, one laundry and a separate post office.

The village nurse and midwife was Nurse Pitman. She was a farmer's wife and lived at Haines Farm, now 'Nods Fold', and later at Shorts Green Farm.

The population was about seven hundred.

Motcombe in 1908 and 1909

UNLIKE 1907 when there were major alterations to the interior of the church, including a new organ, there appears to have been no significant events in Motcombe in 1908 or 1909.

Motcombe House had been unoccupied since 1905 as, due to severe financial problems, Lord Stalbridge, who owned it, could no longer afford to live there and had to make do with his London home in Sussex Gardens. His chairmanship of the London and North Western Railway and some other directorships kept him solvent.

Although he stayed well away from Motcombe, he was very much in evidence elsewhere. Included in his many public engagements was opening the L.& N.W.R's new dock at Garston, Liverpool in 1909 which was named after him. Also in that year he became a vice-president of the League for Opposing Women's Suffrage.

Charles Prideaux, owner of Motcombe factory, had undertaken one of his Lordship's duties by distributing parcels of food to the poor of the village. He could well afford to do so as his business was expanding, particularly the dried milk products with the brand names of 'Casumen' and 'Lacumen', for which he had been awarded some lucrative government contracts.

The Rev. George Bradley Jones was the vicar. He had come to Motcombe in 1904 as successor to the Rev. Tanner.

David Rice, clerk of the works for the Motcombe estate, was chairman of the parish council. He lived at Enmore Green, which was then in the civil as well as the ecclesiastical parish of Motcombe.

Thomas Hiscock, a farmer at Thanes Farm, was the parish clerk. He had been appointed in 1894 when the parish council was first formed.

The main item of business for the parish council at that time was to provide a reading and recreation room at Motcombe. This proved to be a very contentious matter because the Enmore Green councillors did not see why their ratepayers should have to pay for something that would only benefit Motcombe. It was not until 1911 that it was finally resolved not to proceed. Had the proposal gone ahead, it would have been built on or near the site of the present Memorial Hall and been constructed of wood with a corrugated iron roof.

Meshach Moore was then the church parish clerk. He was one of the two village blacksmiths. His father and grandfather before him had also followed that trade and held the office of parish clerk. They too were called Meshach.

4
Events in Motcombe

The Sesquicentenary of St. Mary's Church, Motcombe and its subsequent history until 1883

ON 27th July 1847 the newly rebuilt church of St. Mary's, Motcombe was consecrated by the Bishop of Salisbury, the Rt. Rev. Edward Denison.

The first stone had been laid on 3rd August of the previous year by Lord Richard de Aquila Grosvenor, youngest son of the second Marquess of Westminster, Lord of the Manor of Gillingham and landlord of the Motcombe and Shaftesbury estates, whose Dorset seat was at Motcombe House.

Lord Richard had performed the ceremony in the absence of his parents who were at their London residence, Grosvenor House. They were occupied with social engagements and business matters concerning the Marquess's London estates which he had inherited, together with the main estate in Cheshire, following the death of his father in 1845. Nevertheless they had both taken a keen interest in the rebuilding plans and Lord Westminster had made a substantial contribution of £1000 towards the cost.

Motcombe Church was officially a Chapel of Ease; because Motcombe, although a civil parish, then formed part of the very large ecclesiastical parish of Gillingham, which extended over 15,886 acres and incorporated Milton, East and West Stour, and until 1814, had also included Bourton.

Motcombe's Parish Church therefore was St. Mary's, Gillingham and its Incumbent, the Vicar of Gillingham.

It was not a satisfactory situation; Motcombe itself covered 4780 acres with a population, according to the 1841 census, of 1538.

But matters had improved somewhat in 1843, when it was decided to build a Chapel of Ease at Enmore Green then part of the parish of Motcombe.

However there had been an earlier period when Motcombe had been a separate parish with its own Vicar. In 1646 its parishioners had successfully petitioned the Dorset Standing Committee who decreed that 'the vicarage at Motcombe do henceforth stand distinct and divided from Gillingham and that it remain as a parochial Church of it selfe.'

Unfortunately its time as an independent parish was to be of short duration; after the restoration of the Monarchy it reverted to its formal status and remained so for over two hundred years.

The Old Church or Chapel of Ease

L ITTLE is known of the former church which was taken down when the new one was built on the same site in 1846. Evidence exists that there was a place of worship at Motcombe in 1318, when the first Vicar of Gillingham was instituted; as a stipulation was then made that 'the Vicar should have a house near the Church at Gillingham and assign a house at Motcombe for the priest officiating in that Chapel.'

Whether that chapel was the same one that was pulled down more than five centuries later, or whether there were others in the meantime

The old church or, correctly, chapel of ease

is unknown. It would seem however that the original chapel remained; but was altered and enlarged over the years to accommodate the growing number of worshippers as the population increased; for Motcombe was then included in the Royal Manor and Forest of Gillingham, where clearances and encroachments on the forest were made to provide space for more settlements.

A good idea of what the old building looked like can be obtained from a drawing made in 1829 by J.C.Buckler, an architect, of the 'South East View of Motcombe Church in Dorsetshire.' This view substantiates Hutchins's description of it, in his *History of Dorset*, first edition published 1774, as 'an ancient structure with an embattled tower'. This sketch shows the tower built above the door with the battlements, four finials and a sundial affixed to the wall.

The remains of the old preaching cross can also be seen, situated near the main entrance, where it still stands, although the stump is somewhat shorter.

Preaching crosses were used, as the name implies, to preach from, usually by friars in order that due preparation was made before entering the sacred building. One source dates this cross as late fourteenth century, while another suggests the fifteenth century.

The Rev. Henry Deane

HENRY Deane became Vicar of Gillingham in 1832 and was destined to complete almost fifty years of dedicated ministry before his death in 1882. His administrative abilities proved a great asset in such a large parish. He was particularly noted for his church building and for the development of education; this he did by providing new schools and expanding the existing ones.

The unsatisfactory situation at Enmore Green was soon dealt with when a cottage was converted into a day school. It was also used for Sunday evening services, being first licensed for this purpose in January 1834, nine years before the church was built and a residentiary curate provided.

The New Church at Motcombe

THE first move regarding Motcombe's place of worship came in 1841, when Henry Deane consulted George Alexander, the architect who had built Enmore Green church, with a view to carrying out repairs and

St Mary's Church, Motcombe

improvements. He accordingly drew up plans to give effect to this. Yet, in the following year, a further examination of the church was made and it was decided that a new one should be built in the Early English Style. The architect was then instructed to prepare a design for this. At this stage Earl Grosvenor was also consulted, in all probability on account of the large financial contribution he had agreed to make.

Three years were to elapse before anything further was recorded, when Alexander was called on to design a church this time in the Perpendicular Style to hold 500 persons. However, following an interview with Lord Westminster [the former Earl Grosvenor who had now succeeded to the Marquisate], he was instructed to reduce the size to hold 400 persons. Obviously there was some divergence of view between the Rev. Deane and the Marquess but a compromise was reached at the end of 1845 when plans were made for a church to hold 450 people at a cost not to exceed £2000 which was accepted by both parties.

Now that the style and size of the proposed new church had at last been resolved, the next stage could begin. In April 1846, the architect met the Vicar and the Marquess and received their instructions to draw up the neccessary working plans so that tenders could be submitted. Two months later, the tenders were opened in the presence of the architect, with the result that Uriah Maskell's bid of £1573 5s. was accepted and he was accordingly awarded the contract.

Uriah was a Shaftesbury man by birth, but he had lived in Motcombe since his marriage in 1834.

Before the rebuilding could commence, the agreement of the Vestry had to be obtained. For this purpose a meeting took place on 23 June 1846 with Samuel Ullett, Lord Westminster's land agent in the chair. Not only had the rebuilding to be approved but also a proposal to levy a rate of one shilling in the pound which would raise £326.7.8 to make up the difference in the amount subscribed and the amount required. When the vote was taken there were 41 in favour of the proposals and 23 against, thus demonstrating considerable opposition to the scheme but nevertheless a comfortable majority to enable it to proceed. On the same day the contract was signed, when Uriah Maskell engaged with the Vicar and the two churchwardens to pull down and rebuild the church for an amount of £1573 5s. and to complete the operation by 1st May 1847.

There was some disagreement between Lady Westminster and the Vicar concerning the alternative arrangements for the church services during the rebuilding period. Her Ladyship had suggested, much to the consternation of the Vicar and the Bishop, that permission should be sought from the Wesleyans to use their chapel for this purpose. The Bishop, in a letter to the Rev. Deane, expressed his displeasure at this proposal considering it tantamount to approving dissent, and stated his willingness to write to Lord Westminster himself about her Ladyship's suggestion if necessary. Although this showed little ecumenical spirit, it was perhaps understandable. Motcombe was then a Methodist stronghold. John Wesley had preached here in 1779 and the chapel was reputed to have been the first in a Dorset village. The Primitive Methodists too, had become numerically strong enough in 1828 to build their own chapel. By 1846, the Dissenters had outnumbered the Anglicans and were continuing to increase. Lady Westminster's suggestion may well have been made because she did not want her new school to be used for this purpose. The Marchioness of Westminster's School, as it was called, had been built by the Westminsters in 1839 and was entirely maintained by them. However, in the end it was used for the services but the Westminsters, when staying at Motcombe House, chose not to worship in the school but attended either Holy Trinity church at Shaftesbury or St. John's at Enmore Green. During the rebuilding period there were eleven christenings, eighteen burials and fourteen marriages. Services for christenings and burials could be held in unconsecrated buildings provided permission from the diocesan authorities had been obtained but marriages could not. These were all solemnised at St. Rumbold's Church, Cann, by Motcombe's curate the Rev. Peter Rideout. The question arises why St. John's church at Enmore Green, being the nearest and within the same parish was not used. The most likely explanation is that if it had been, the resident curate might have demanded to perform the ceremonies and have the fee. Curates were usually poorly paid and it is known that the Rev. Rideout had financial problems; therefore the Rector of Cann had consented to the use of his church to help his impecunious colleague.

The new church was completed in accordance with the terms of the contract but, as usual, there were extras which brought the final total to £1901 19s. 6d. Everything now appeared to be ready for the consecration, but a most important requirement had been omitted: a faculty, the ecclesiastical equivalent of planning permission, had not been obtained.

Motcombe Vicarage after enlargement, about 1883

The explanation for this is that Gillingham was a Peculiar, originally a Royal Peculiar, in the days when the Manor and Forest of Gillingham belonged to the Sovereign. The distinction had continued after the Forest and Manor had been sold by Charles I. As a Peculiar it was outside the jurisdiction of the Bishop. In Gillingham's case the jurisdiction was exerised by the Lord of the Manor, who appointed an official to act on his behalf. The appointee at this time was the Rev. William Patteson, Rector of St. James' Church, Shaftesbury.

In a document dated 29th April 1846, William Patteson, 'Official of the Peculiar of Gillingham and Ordinary thereof', had given his consent to the taking down and rebuilding of Motcombe Church which normally would have been sufficient, but an Order in Council dated 23rd August 1846 had abolished Peculiars in the Salisbury diocese which meant that Gillingham now came within the jurisdiction of the Bishop. This would most certainly have created many problems. One was whether the authority granted by William Patteson was still valid, or whether a faculty was now required. The latter must have been the case, because the following action was taken: the Vicar petitioned the Rev. Patteson, still addressing him as the 'Official lawfully constituted of the Peculiar and exempt jurisdiction of Gillingham', stating that he had omitted to obtain a Licence and Faculty and prayed that he [Patteson] would be pleased to grant one. The answer came in the form of a proclamation dated 1st July 1847 although addressed by Patteson to the Vicar it had been signed at Salisbury by the Registrar of the Diocese. It stated that a Licence and Faculty would be granted provided there were no objections from the parishioners. To this end a copy of the proclamation had to be affixed to the principal outer door of Gillingham, Motcombe and Enmore Green Churches on Sunday 4th July 1847 to enable any parishioner to exercise their right of objection. There being no objections, the Licence and Faculty were accordingly granted.

The role of the Rev. Patteson therefore, although still referred to by his old title, was now that of a Surrogate and it was in that capacity that he attended the consecration of the church three weeks later in the absence of the Chancellor of the Diocese.

Lady Westminster and the Curates

ALTHOUGH Motcombe now had a new church, nothing else appears to have changed until the death of the Rev. Rideout in 1850 after serving 42 years as curate.

Records show that there had been a parsonage at Motcombe at least until the end of the seventeenth century, but there had ceased to be one, or in use as such, by Rideout's time. He had formerly lived at Pensbury House, just within the parish and about two miles from the church. In about 1838 he moved to a house in Shaftesbury.

The Rev. James Warrington Rogers was the next curate. He too resided outside the parish at Newbury in Gillingham. This was of some concern to the Westminsters who considered that the shepherd should live among his flock. This came about, however, in 1860 when a new parsonage was built in the village near the church and school, although there are indications that Rogers had been living in Motcombe prior to moving into his new home. He and his family continued to live

The Rev Canon G B Oldfield, curate of Motcombe 1867-71

there until 1867 when he left to become curate at Stour Provost. Rogers' chief fault, in the eyes of the Westminsters, was that he had been influenced by the Oxford Movement and practised what Lady Westminster called 'High Church Tricks' which led to their complaining to the Vicar. What the Rev. Deane's reaction was is not known, but it is said that he was not averse to High Church practices and may well have advised his Curate to exercise discretion when these two influential persons attended church.

The High Church curate's successor was the Rev. George Oldfield whose curacy carried a stipend of £100 per annum with the stipulation that he reside in the chapelry of Motcombe.

Oldfield clearly found favour with Lady Westminster who, after the Marquess's death in 1869, had inherited his Dorset and Wiltshire estates. When, three years later, the living in the adjacent parish of Sedgehill became vacant, her Ladyship, in whose gift it was, offered it to Oldfield who, no doubt gladly accepted, as the net stipend was £300 per annum plus the house.

But for the Rev. Alfred Elton who followed him at Motcombe, it was a different story: In her estimation, he was a failure as a minister. His sermons were variously described as 'vapid; somniferous; too long and totally useless'. Also on one occasion she complained that he and Meshach Moore [the parish clerk] had run a race in the creed to see as to whom could gabble to the end the quicker. His greatest failing however, in her veiw, was that he did not do enough for the sick and the poor. This duty was of paramount inportance to her and her own record in this regard was excellent. Despite his apparent failings he survived four years, resigning his curacy to accept the living of Pitminster in Somerset.

By contrast, the Rev. William Carpendale, who succeeded him, met with the noble lady's approval. He preached good sermons, was anxious to help those in need and was liked by the congregation. Sadly three years later things had changed,the congregation had dwindled to about twenty, most of whom were Lady Westminster's servants. This was due to Carpendale's misconduct, the nature of which is not known but must have been serious, for he was obliged to resign and leave the village. His replacement, the Rev. Arthur Perceval was a misfit; he did not like Motcombe or his flock, nor was he liked by them. He left after a few months much to the relief of Lady Westminster and the parishioners.

Then came the Rev. Cecil Brereton who was to be Motcombe's last curate. He was still a deacon when he first arrived but about four months later was ordained priest. Despite his lack of experience as a minister, the octogenarian dowager was well disposed towards him and regarded him as her protegé. His departure in the summer of 1883 co-incided with an important change in Motcombe's ecclesiastical history.

Motcombe becomes a Separate Parish

H ENRY Deane died on 6 April 1882. There seems to have been a tacit agreement that after his demise, Motcombe, with Enmore Green, would become a separate parish.

Lady Westminster was saddened by the death of an old friend of fifty years standing, yet she lost no time in writing a tactfully worded letter to the Bishop for confirmation that this was still the case and expressed her wish to be consulted before an incumbent was appointed. The Bishop's reply was non-committal; nevertheless an Order in Council dated 23rd August 1883 authorised the creation of a new ecclesiastical parish of Motcombe with Enmore Green and on 30th November of that year Lady Westmister's nominee, the Rev. Canon John Smith, was collated and inducted as first Vicar, or to be precise, Perpetual Curate.

Smith's last parish had been Lyme Regis but at one time he was Rector of Kington Magna and Rural Dean of Shaftesbury. In 1882 he had been made an honorary Canon of Salisbury Cathedral.

Her Ladyship was convinced that he was the right man for Motcombe and through her powerful influence had secured his appointment. As an inducement she had also agreed to augment his stipend by £200 per annum.

So at last the succession of Curates had ended and Motcombe had its own Vicar and its own parish church. Enmore Green still retained its Curate. Moreover the dowager Marchioness proved to be right in her choice. In the following year her daughter, Lady Theodora Guest, attended both the morning and evening services at Motcombe. She remarked on the excellence of Canon Smith's preaching and the size of the congregation, particularly at the evening service which was crowded such as she had never seen before. Four years later Lady Westminster, then aged ninety, expressed her satisfaction with her Vicar in a letter to a friend. She wrote: 'We are happy in having here the most excellent clergyman I ever met with. He knows and visits every person in the parish with kindness and goodness and perfect judgement to all which saves me all trouble and anxiety. I know that every individual is known and well attended to, much better than I ever could.'

A 150th Anniversary

THERE was great rejoicing in Gillingham on 2nd May 1859 when the railway from Salisbury and the station were opened.

Although it was a weekday (Monday) large numbers of people from the surrounding area converged on the town which had been decorated with flags, banners and triumphal arches bearing appropriate wording for the occasion.

Two large tents sufficient to accommodate about 2500 had been erected to provide the 'labouring classes' of the parish, gratis, with tea and cakes or bread, beef and beer.

Sports were held in a nearby field and dancing to the music of two bands.

There was good cause for rejoicing as it was realised that the railway would bring many benefits to Gillingham and the locality.

The twenty-two miles of single track had been completed in three years. Besides Gillingham there were four other stations en route: Semley, Tisbury, Dinton and Wilton. Apart from the freight trains there were four passenger trains each way on weekdays and three on Sundays. The journey time from Gillingham to Salisbury was fifty minutes and from Semley forty minutes. Passengers changed at Salisbury for Waterloo with a twenty minute wait. This journey took 2 hours 35 minutes.

In 1860 the single line was extended to Sherborne. The construction of the line caused many inconveniences, principally the loss of land. Several Motcombe farmers were affected in this way. One example was the embankment between the Semley road near Knapp and Corner Lane which resulted in a field called Keintons being severely reduced in size.

Two bridges had to be built, one to make an archway under the embankment near Corner Lane and the other over the line at

Coppleridge. This was then a turnpike road between Shaftesbury and Mere.

The line crossed at least three footpaths, one being over the previously mentioned embankment resulting in a steep climb to cross the line and a sharp descent on the other side.

James Bartley was one of those who prospered during the building period. He lived near the line at Corner Lane and obtained a licence to sell beer at his home. Doubtless he did very well from the navvies who posed problems in the areas where they worked due to their unruly behaviour mainly caused by drunkenness resulting in harm to persons and property.

When the factory began operations, efforts were made to have a station at Motcombe but this was turned down. Another request by the parish council in 1901 was again refused.

There were celebrations in Gillingham on 2nd May 2009 to mark this anniversary with stalls and sideshows in the station area. Also the Mayor and dignitaries, led by the town band and town crier, went in procession to the station where the official opening ceremony took place at 11.30am.

The Golden Jubilee of 1887

THE last golden jubilee of a reigning monarch, prior to the present, was that of Queen Victoria in 1887. In Motcombe the occasion was marked by a church service in the morning which was well attended. The vicar, the Rev. Canon Smith, preached a touching and eloquent service in praise of the Queen. The Lydlinch band was in attendance although they played outside.

In the afternoon a fête was held in the cricket field (the field behind the old workhouse) where Lady Westminster presented jubilee medals to over two hundred children. Then some several hundred of Motcombe's inhabitants partook of a substantial tea provided by the farmers who presided at the tables.

This was followed by sports, the winners receiving their prizes from Lady Westminster assisted by her daughter and son-in-law, Lady Theodora and Mr. Merthyr Guest.

Finally came the dancing accompanied by the band, which continued until ten o'clock when the proceedings closed with hearty cheers for Her Majesty.

To commemorate this jubilee Motcombe gave a ring of six new bells to the church. Four were from the parishioners and two, the heaviest, from Lady Theodora Guest. They were not hung in time to ring for the jubilee but rang for the first time on the 8 November of that year to celebrate Lady Westminster's ninetieth birthday, when there were again celebrations in the village.

Motcombe Parish Council Centenary

PARISH and District Councils were established by the Local Government Act of 1894. Hitherto, parishes had been governed and rated by the Vestry, an unelected body of ratepayers based on the Church, whose powers were taken over by the new parish councils, leaving them responsible only for Church affairs. Ten years previously, the Third Reform Act had extended the franchise to householders and lodgers in rural areas. The new Act gave women the right to vote and stand as candidates, provided they had the same voting qualifications, but only in parish and district council elections.

The Parish of Motcombe, which included Enmore Green and Sherborne Causeway, had 292 names on its electoral role in 1894, 38 of whom were women.

In order to prepare the Motcombe electors for the powers they were shortly to enjoy, Lord Stalbridge, the owner of the Motcombe estate, convened a meeting. This took place in the boys' school (the present school building dated 1874) on 12 October 1894, when Henry Hobhouse, Liberal MP for East Somerset and an authority on local government, gave a talk explaining in detail how the parish councils would operate. He also described the procedures that would have to be adopted at the inaugural parish meeting. It was reported that the room was full and that the audience had followed the speaker with the greatest attention so that they were ready for the great day – 4 December 1894 – the date of the first parish meeting. This was an historic occasion, not only in Motcombe but in rural areas throughout England and Wales, when about seven thousand civil parishes came into being. For the first time ever, a democratically elected body was to govern the parish. It marked the beginning of a new era. Many had high hopes and great expectations.

The First Meeting and Elections

THE meeting was a lively affair. About a hundred electors were present: a reasonably good attendance, considering the time of year, the lack of transport for many, and the scattered nature of the parish.

Lord Stalbridge was unanimously elected to chair the proceedings which were therefore carried out strictly in accordance with the statutory requirements. There were over twenty valid nominations for the eleven places, thus necessitating a vote, which was conducted by a show of hands, resulting in equal voting for the eleventh place between Hubert Woodford and George Gatehouse. The Chairman gave his casting vote in favour of the former but George Gatehouse objected and demanded a poll. The Chairman then declared the meeting closed.

Polling took place on 17 December, the same date as the elections for the new District Council. Voting was by secret ballot with polling stations at Enmore Green and Motcombe. As a result, the following were elected and became Motcombe's first Parish Councillors:

Nathanial BENJAFIELD	108	35	Shorts Green Farm	Cattle and pig breeder Farmer
Edwin FRANCIS	84	20	Motcombe	Gardener on Estate
George GATEHOUSE	124	31	Enmore Green	Auctioneer
Clarence HARRIS	102	35	Motcombe	Carpenter and Builder
Edwin INKPEN	94	36	Motcombe	Farmer and Innkeeper, The Royal Oak
Henry MARSH	81	28	Enmore Green	Agricultural Labourer
Edwin MILES	91	42	Nettlebed, Motcombe	Nuseryman
Frederick PICKFORD	81	35	Enmore Green	Innkeeper, The Fountain
Charles PRIDEAUX	152	58	Motcombe	Dairy produce merchant, Farmer

Henry THOMPSON	78	36	Motcombe	General Labourer at Motcombe Factory
Osmund WOODFORD	80	38	Cowherd Shute Farm	Farmer

The first column of figures denotes the votes cast in the poll; the second, those by a show of hands. It was an astute move on the part of George Gatehouse as he had quadrupled his vote. No doubt he received much more support from the Enmore Green electors who had not been able to attend the parish meeting because of the distance. The secret ballot would have encouraged those who were wary of voting publicly by a show of hands.

All the elected councillors had increased their vote: six had done so by publishing election addresses in the local newspaper. Two who had been elected at the parish meeting failed in the ballot. They were the Vicar, the Rev. Sidney Dugdale, and Arthur Hiscock of Manor Farm. It is significant to note that three councillors – Francis, Marsh and Thompson – were from the 'labouring classes' as they were then called. Two labourers and a gardener, hitherto without status, would now have a say in the government of the parish. Regrettably, Marsh had to be disqualified for a time as he had been in receipt of parish relief, but was unanimously re-elected by his fellow councillors the following August.

The First Council Meeting

THE birthday of Motcombe Parish Council is 31 December 1894 when the newly-elected councillors came into office and had their first meeting. With Charles Prideaux in the chair, the parish fathers settled down to business. Firstly they had to elect a chairman who could either be chosen from their own number or be a person outside the council who was qualified to be so. They opted for the latter and elected Lord Stalbridge. As a Peer of the Realm, his Lordship was precluded from voting in Parliamentary elections but was entitled to vote in all local elections and to become a councillor. At that time he was Deputy Chairman of the Dorset County Council and, also, Chairman of the London and North Western Railway.

Charles Prideaux, who had topped the poll, was elected as Vice-Chairman. His factory in the village was by then well established and his business was rapidly expanding. He had another factory at Stalbridge and a combined workforce in the region of seventy. The office of Treasurer went to Clarence Harris, a member of his father's building firm which was currently engaged with others in building a new Motcombe House (now Port Regis School) for Lord Stalbridge.

An essential position to be filled and a new creation was that of clerk to the new civil parish. Thomas Hiscock, former collector of the poor rate in the time of the Vestry, was appointed to that office, a position he was to hold for twenty-five years. His salary was later fixed at £30 per annum. Other matters were deferred to the next meeting, held on 11 January 1895 when Lord Stalbridge was in the chair.

And Then . . .

THE council met no fewer than fifteen times during its busy first year, 1895, alternating between Motcombe and Enmore Green. Ad hoc committees were set up to deal with the provision of allotments and the water supply at Enmore Green. Lord Westminister had laid on a water supply for Motcombe but, in Enmore Green, the inhabitants must have been drinking 'flavoured' water. Tramps had been seen washing in it, and animals drinking from it. Endless arguments followed over footpath and road standards, loose animals, and all the other problems still being dealt with by the Council.

In April 1933, Enmore Green was transferred to the care of Shaftesbury Borough, followed in 1985 by Littledown, although in 1989 Motcombe gained the whole of Kingsettle Woods to the A350.

During the two World Wars, the Council organised protection for the residents and went on fire watching duties. Many generous people gave their time and talents to ensure that life would go on as the people of Motcombe wanted it.

In the first one hundred years, there have been eighteen chairmen and just six clerks.

Extraordinary and Unprecedented Scene at Motcombe Parish Meeting
Two Prominent Councillors Come to Blows

FIRSTLY, it must be said that this unfortunate incident did not occur in recent years. In fact, it happened in 1911. The combatants were Arthur Hiscock (Motcombe) and George Ranger (Enmore Green).

The cause of the fracas was the proposed building of a room for use as a Reading Room or Working Men's Club at Motcombe. The proposal had originated in 1906, when a Parish Meeting had authorised the Parish Council to accept an offer from Lord Stalbridge of a piece of land for this purpose. During the next few years (things moved very slowly in Motcombe in those days) various complications arose, and matters came to a head at the above meeting held at Enmore Green on 23 October 1911. At that time meetings were held alternately at Motcombe and Enmore Green.

The meeting was called to rescind the minute of 1906 in favour of a Reading Room, because Enmore Green Ratepayers did not see why they should help to pay for something that would be of little or no use to them. Originally they had agreed because then it had meant only a 1d rate would have to be imposed, but this had now increased to 3d.

It was a packed meeting; many had to stand outside. Cllr Hiscock put his case for the Room, and Cllr Ranger the case against. When the vote came, not surprisingly as most of those attending were from Enmore Green, there was a large majority against. Cllr Ranger then thanked the voters for their support. It was at this stage that the trouble began. Cllr Hiscock shouted 'Shut your mouth' and sang the National Anthem, completely drowning Cllr Ranger's speech. This led to a heated altercation, resulting in blows being struck despite efforts to restrain them. This incident is without parallel in the history of Motcombe Parish Council, and was not recorded in the minutes.

In 1933 the Parish boundaries were redrawn and Enmore Green left Motcombe and joined Shaftesbury.

Who were the two councillors who so disgraced themselves and caused so much publicity?

George Ranger lived at Enmore Green. He was a postman and a chapel-goer. Described as being 'a bit of a spitfire' by temperament, he was nevertheless a very able councillor.

Arthur Hiscock of Manor Farm, Motcombe, had been Chairman of the Council from 1906-1909. He was a prominent figure locally, serving on several public bodies. His success as a cattle and pig breeder had earned him an international reputation. He had won many championships at agricultural shows throughout the country, and was a member of the Council of the Royal Agricultural Society. Pedigree Shorthorn cattle and Berkshire pigs from his Motcombe farm were exported to many countries, including Australia, the USA, Russia and South Africa for breeding purposes.

It is not known if the two councillors made it up later, but both continued on the Parish Council.

The Seventy-Fifth Anniversary of Motcombe Memorial Hall

THE year 2000 was the seventy fifth anniversary of the opening of the Memorial Hall. In 1925 Lady Stalbridge had laid the foundation stone at a ceremony held on Sunday 22 November when a procession had formed at the church consisting of the Choir, Churchwardens, the Vicar, (the Rev. E.C. King) the Bishop of Sherborne and her Ladyship. After an impressive service, the Bishop blessed the stone which was then put in place.

It had the following inscription:- 'In memory of Richard De Acquila [the correct spelling should be Aquila], first Baron Stalbridge, Born January 28 1837 died May 18 1912. This stone was laid by Gladys Elizabeth, wife of the second Baron Stalbridge November 22 1925.'

Motcombe Choral Society outside the new Memorial Hall, about 1930

Lady Stalbridge also performed the opening ceremony which took place on 11 June 1928 in the presence of a large gathering including members of the Grosvenor family. There were several speeches one by Charles Prideaux, proprietor of Motcombe factory, who had been responsible for raising the money for the building which had cost £1522.

Lord Stalbridge was not present at either ceremony. He did however contribute £200 towards the cost and also gave the land on which the hall was built.

The Stalbridges had left Motcombe after the estate was sold in 1925. When Lady Stalbridge died in 1960 she bequeathed £300 towards the maintenance of the hall.

The list of subscribers shows a donation of £50 from the London and North Western Railway of which the first Baron had been chairman and £25 from the Duke of Westminster who was his great nephew. There were generous donations too from some other Grosvenors.

After seventy-five years Motcombe can still boast a fine village hall and is likely to do so for many years to come, serving as a lasting memorial to the first Baron Stalbridge who was described by Charles Prideaux as, 'one of the best gentlemen who ever walked the streets of Motcombe, a kind-hearted gentleman who had a loving smile and a nod for everyone'.

Motcombe Women's Institute Seventy-Fifth Anniversary

MOTCOMBE W.I.'s seventy fifth anniversary was celebrated in style in Motcombe Memorial Hall on 12 October 2005. Tables laid with cloths and serviettes alternating the W.I colours of red and green made a welcoming sight with flower arrangements which would be given later as free raffle prizes. Past and present members and guests enjoyed the wine and cold buffet prepared by the committee and two co-opted members and all members contributed towards the cost. It was followed by popular music of the 1930s and a witty commentary presented by David Andrews. A vote of thanks for a splendid evening was given by a retired V.O.C and a lovely arrangement of flowers was presented to the president by the secretary on behalf of everybody present. A happy event enjoyed by all with many letters of appreciation received afterwards echoing these sentiments.

The inaugural meeting took place in the Memorial Hall on 5 December 1930 when fifty members were enrolled with an annual subscription of two shillings (10p). This was later increased to half a crown (12½p).

In the following January the newly formed W.I held their first New Year's party. By then the membership had risen to sixty-one. At that time it was the only organisation in the village exclusively for women

Some members of Motcombe Women's Institute, about 1935

and proved to be a great success with a steadily increasing membership which, within ten years, had exceeded a hundred.

Their first big venture was the creation of the 'Jubilee Corner'. The members worked hard for several months in making a plot of land near the hall into a pretty garden with flowers, shrubs and rockeries. A house 'Broadoak' now stands on this site. It was officially opened in July 1936 when a fete was held in the recreation ground funded entirely by the members.

At Christmas time there was a party for the children. This was a great occasion and much enjoyed by the youngsters.

Meetings were held regularly throughout the war years. In addition to the usual programme, the members were occupied in knitting comforts for the forces and other appropriate activities. The children's parties still continued despite the rationing to which the evacuees were also invited.

Since the war there has been a decline in the membership but this is a national trend and not confined to Motcombe.

A sad event occurred in 1968 when a pipe burst in the hall resulting in the W.I records being destroyed. Despite this mishap a beautiful book of memorabilia of Motcombe W.I was produced by a member for the sixtieth anniversary in 1990. In that year to celebrate this occasion two trees were planted in the recreation ground. Also in 1990, a book 'Hidden Dorset' was published by the Dorset Federation of Women's

Institutes, compiled from information sent by Institutes in the county. It is pleasing to note that Motcombe was one of the contributors.

The main purpose of the Women's Institute is 'to improve and develop conditions of rural life by providing a centre for educational and social intercourse and activities'. Motcombe W.I has certainly fulfilled their aims in the past seventy five years and can be proud of its achievements.

5
Motcombe Buildings

Three Motcombe Pubs

THE two past ones were 'The Bull Inn' and 'The New Inn'. Information is scant regarding the former, but it is known that it was situated in The Street, in what is now part of the garden of 'Brookside'. It was therefore most likely to have been the thatched house which stood there, remembered only by older Motcombe people, as it was pulled down in the 1930's, long after its days as a public house had ended. There is evidence that it had definitely ceased to be 'The Bull' by 1836 and indications are that it had become a private house in the 1820s.

The Motcombe Overseers of the Poor held a meeting here in 1813 and charged the cost of their liquid refreshment to the Parish.

The former Primitive Methodist Chapel. The thatched cottage next to it, of which a corner is visible, was probably once the Bull Inn

A little more is known of 'The New Inn'. It was built in about 1825 by two Motcombe farmers – John Pond of Dunedge Lodge and Thomas Pond of Northayes on land they had bought at Bittles Green. The date and name suggest that it was the successor of 'The Bull'.

It appears that its time as an inn was of short duration, but again it has not been established exactly when this ended. Certainly by 1840, when it was known as Pond's House and was used as the farmhouse for Frog Lane Farm after it had burnt down about three years previously.

Thirty years later it became the home of Mrs. Alfred King, widow of the head gamekeeper of the Motcombe Estate. Here one could get a meat dinner for 2½d, subsidised by the Lady of the Manor – the Dowager Marchioness of Westminster.

Towards the end of the last century it was converted into a laundry, run by Mrs Lucy Jones. She was followed by Charles Legg who, when the laundry closed, started a car hire business. During the Second World War it reverted to a private residence, and continues to be so – now called 'Frog House'.

In 1840 the Royal Oak was one of four beerhouses in Motcombe. The licensee, or beer retailer, was Charles Green. After his death his widow, Martha, took over. She was succeeded by her son-in-law, John Broadway, who had married her youngest daughter Sarah. (John was a direct descendant of the Broadways whose large tomb can be seen in front of St Mary's Church.) He was by trade a builder and carpenter and it was he who built the 'Royal Oak' in 1870 when the old one, which had stood close by, was demolished.

Although the landlord had built his own pub, the cost was not to his account, for at the time it belonged to the Motcombe Estate.

Motcombe's 'local' was a superior building resembling a hotel, both in size and style. This is what it was intended to be and was, in its early days, known as The Royal Oak Hotel.

The Head Gamekeeper's House and Kennels

IN 1831 Robert, first Marquess of Westminster, then Lord of the Manor, gave Motcombe House to his eldest son Richard, third Earl Grosvenor. Then four years later the Marquess handed over the Motcombe estate to his son. One of the several improvements that the Earl made was to provide a better home and kennels for the head gamekeeper. The site chosen was near Dunedge Lodge Farm. The house, which was constructed of stone with a slate roof, was a substantial building and quite spacious for that period. The kennels for the game dogs were built close by.

Lot Pitman, 1863-1945, gamekeeper on the Motcombe estate

The builder was Richard Downs of Shaftesbury who had also made extensive alterations to Motcombe House.

Nearly forty years later, in about 1874, the Dowager Marchioness of Westminster, then the Lady of the Manor, decided to build a new house and kennels for the head gamekeeper. It is now 'Cliff House' near Thanes Farm.

Again it was a Shaftesbury builder, Thomas Miles. He built several houses in Motcombe and Frog Lane Farm, also the 1874 school building.

The former gamekeeper's house was then called the 'Old Kennels' and still is, which gives the wrong impression that it was the previous home of the South West Wilts Hunt. They were originally

The Old Kennels, Motcombe, the first gamekeeper's house built in the 1830s

The former head gamekeeper's house

at Sutton Veny, near Warminster. When Lord Stalbridge became Master of the Hunt he decided to have the employees and foxhounds closer to him at Motcombe House, which he did in about 1920 when the present kennels were built.

Motcombe's Shop and Post Office

MOTCOMBE is fortunate in that it still has a village shop and post office. There has been a shop on this site for over a hundred and sixty years but the post office was originally at the house now appropriately called 'The Old Post House'.

It was opened in about 1870 and Thomas Parsons was the first sub-postmaster (the main office was at Shaftesbury). He was a carpenter in the family business of builders so his wife ran the post office as well as a general store.

When Thomas Parsons died in 1903, his daughter, Elizabeth, who had worked in the post office, was appointed sub-postmistress and her husband, Henry Stainer took over the building firm. At that time four telegram boys were employed who delivered around ninety telegrams a day.

Mrs. Stainer retired in 1955 after completing nearly seventy years in Motcombe post office and fifty-two as sub-post mistress. She died in January 1962 at the age of eighty-nine.

Not long after her retirement the post office was transferred to its present site. William Blandford was the first shopkeeper here and is shown in the 1841 census as a grocer. The shop continued in the family until the beginning of the last century when it was bought by William Shute and was then called 'Shute's Stores'.

Howard Hayden succeeded him in 1930 followed by Edwin Bartlett and then Charles Inglefield, who took over the post office.

During the course of its existence various alterations and additions have been made to the shop and house which most likely began as a small thatched cottage. The part of the building facing north was once two one-bedroom cottages.

Shute's Stores

Further research has revealed that there was a shop on this site in 1830. Elizabeth Blandford was then the shopkeeper, so it was in the ownership of the Blandfords for at least seventy years.

The shop with post office is now run as a community project

The Tap Houses

THERE were at least four tap houses in Motcombe which were probably built as pump houses when the initial water system in Lord Westminster's time came into use. It seems likely that taps replaced the pumps with the improvements carried out later by Lady Westminster.

A restored taphouse, now a bus shelter

One of the tap houses was at North End which has now been restored by the Parish Council. The other three were in the village. One of which, at The Forge, was not a separate building but a recess in the wall and is now bricked up.

The other two were similar to each other in design. One was at Bittles Green: a house now occupies the site on which it stood. The other, opposite the Old Post House, has survived, minus its original roof and has been put to good use as a bus shelter. It has now been restored by the Parish Council.

The Royal Oak

AFTER over 140 years as Motcombe's pub The Royal Oak has now been closed. For most of that time it was the only licensed house in the village. It was built in 1870 to replace an old beerhouse with the same name that had stood close by.

The builder was John Broadway, who became the first licensee. He has previously been licensee of the old beerhouse which he had taken over on the death of his mother-in-law, Martha Green.

Like most of the properties in the village The Royal Oak belonged to the Motcombe estate whose owner was then the Dowager Marchioness of Westminster.

It was a superior building for a village public house in those days, very spacious with six bedrooms and four attic bedrooms so several guests could be accommodated, hence it became known as The Royal Oak Hotel. There were also farm buildings on the site enabling the licensee to keep a few cows and pigs.

John Broadway's time at the new Royal Oak was a very sad one. Here he lost four of his seven children through various illnesses and was twice widowed. His first wife probably had had experience in running a public house as her mother and stepfather had kept the old Royal Oak.

Possibly on account of these bereavements, in about 1877 John decided to move to West Knoyle and take up farming. But here he was again widowed twice and outlived his fourth wife by six years.

Edwin Inkpen became the next tenant and was described in the trade directories as an innkeeper and farmer. His tenancy lasted about twenty-five years when The Royal Oak was taken over by The Dorset Public House Trust Co Ltd and was run by managers.

The Royal Oak in the days when it was the village pub

They were succeeded by The People's Refreshment House Association Ltd, a subsidiary of Charringtons who, when the estate was sold in 1925, were granted a twenty-one years' lease on the premises, but the farm buildings were sold to Charles Prideaux, the owner of Motcombe factory.

Stephen Brighty was then the manager followed by Harry Randall, who is still remembered, so too is Barry Ford who was his successor.

When the lease expired or perhaps before, the P.R.H.A must have bought the pub because in 1956 it was sold by them to Hall and Woodhouse and thus had been one of their houses for over fifty years.

The Royal Oak as a Venue

IN its early years the Royal Oak was the venue for the annual celebrations of the Motcombe New Friendly Society. 'New' because in 1872 it had been reconstituted but had been in existence for many years prior to this.

Club day, as it was known, took place at Whitsuntide and was a big event in the village. The members assembled at the Royal Oak in the morning and formed a procession then, headed by a brass band and the society's banner (which can now be seen in the Memorial Hall), they proceeded to the vicarage to meet the vicar who joined the procession to the church where a special service was held. Afterwards the procession reformed. They then made a few calls on prominent parishioners before returning to the Royal Oak to enjoy a good meal in a marquee when speeches were made and toasts drunk. The rest of the day was usually spent in games and sports.

Another club which had its headquarters at the Royal Oak was the Slate club. It was originally called the Royal Oak Slate and Sick Club but later was renamed The Acorn Slate Club. The main difference between a friendly society and a slate club was that at the end of the year a slate club shared out its surplus funds so that the New Year began with a clean sheet. The share out took place near Christmas and was called share out night when a good time was had by all. Motcombe's Slate Club survived long after the friendly society had ceased to function.

The small village societies were superseded by the much larger organisations such as the Oddfellows, Foresters and the Sons of Temperance, all of these and others were well represented in Motcombe.

Regrettably the date when the slate club wound up is not known but it was still operating in 1958 when Harry Russell, who had been the chairman for 25 years, died.

Another event which involved the Royal Oak was the Bonfire Carnival which was on or near the 5 November. It started in 1898 but did not survive long. The procession of horse drawn floats and a band began from the Royal Oak and finished there. It was followed by a firework display in a field belonging to the pub.

Motcombe football team in 1950 were also patrons of the Royal Oak

Motcombe House

OTCOMBE House [Port Regis School] was built as a new home for Lord Richard De Aquila Grosvenor, First Baron Stalbridge, who inherited the Motcombe and Shaftesbury estates in 1891, following the death of his mother, the dowager Marchioness of Westminster.

The architects were Sir Ernest George and Harold Peto, the former in particular specialised in designing country houses. He was also the architect for the Royal Exchange building in London, Claridges Hotel and Golders Green Crematorium and others. Edwin Lutyens was one of his pupils.

Motcombe House is a characteristic work of Sir George. It is in the Elizabethan style, of red brick with Ham Hill dressings. It is said that a million bricks were used in its construction.

The main contractors were Parnell & Co. of Rugby and the estimated cost £50,000 but it is believed that the figure was nearer £60,000 when completed. One of the builders was Arthur Harris, known as 'Bumpy' Harris. He lived in Motcombe and later built the 'The Grange' (now retirement homes) with stone from the old Motcombe House.

Motcombe House, now Port Regis School

Work on the mansion began in 1893 and was completed in 1895. The old house was then demolished. During the process a workman was killed and several were injured when part of a wall fell on them. The stables, however, as can be seen, were left; they had only been built about twenty years previously to provide accommodation for Lady Theodora Grosvenor's [later Guest] hunters. She lived at the old Motcombe House with her mother.

Why did Lord Stalbridge go to such great expense to build a new mansion when the old one would have been adequate? One reason advanced was that the drains were bad and Lord Stalbridge had contracted typhoid fever. Another was that the old mansion was not good enough for Lady Stalbridge. But whatever the reason, it proved to be a most unwise step because by 1905 Lord Stalbridge could no longer afford to live there and moved to his house in London to live in much reduced circumstances although Motcombe House was not sold.

This disaster was occasioned by the bankruptcy of Lord Sudeley a Liberal colleague. Lord Stalbridge was the principal creditor to the tune of £100,000. Although not bankrupted himself, he suffered a grievous loss. Fortunately he was chairman of the L.& N.W.R. railway and held other directorships and so had some income.

After his death in 1912, his eldest son Hugh inherited the estates and lived at Motcombe House. Although his father had made great sacrifices to keep the estates for his son and heir, Hugh sold Motcombe in 1925 (Shaftesbury and Stalbridge had already been sold). Motcombe House, however, remained unsold and was threatened with demolition but for the action of Charles Prideaux, owner of Motcombe dairy factory, who bought it because it is said he could not bear the thought of it being demolished.

This was in 1929 but the house remained unoccupied until the war when it was let to the Consolidated Gold Fields of South Africa, a firm which had evacuated from London. After the war it came into the possession of Port Regis School.

6
Church and Chapel

Motcombe Church Bells

IN 1552 an inventory taken of Motcombe church shows that there were four bells in the belfry. However the four bells that were taken down in 1887 were not the original ones; for they bore dates of 1620, 1660, 1688 and 1705.

In 1887, Queen Victoria's Golden Jubilee, Motcombe decided to commemorate the occasion by having six new bells. Four, costing £145 were donated by the parishioners, and the other two, the heaviest, by Lady Theodora Guest. These cost £141. Other expenditure was for a new floor; cocoa matting and a lamp for the belfry. Also the ringers of St. James's, Shaftesbury, were paid £1 10s. for teaching the Motcombe ringers.

Mr. Merthyr Guest, Lady Theodora's husband, bought the old bells for £45. The new bells were rung for the first time on 8 November 1887, Lady Westminster's (the Lady of the manor) ninetieth birthday.

In 1935, a quarter peal of Grandsire Doubles (1260 changes) was rung by Motcombe ringers and in 1947 a full peal (5040 changes) was rung by the Salisbury Diocesan Guild of Ringers. The team included one Motcombe man, Robert Wareham. Miss Gillian Edwards, niece of the celebrated ringer Rev. Frank Llewellyn Edwards of Kington Magna was also in the team.

Motcombe Methodists

THE year 1992 marked the sixtieth anniversary of the Methodist Union. Before 1932 there were two chapels in Motcombe – the Primitive and the Wesleyan. Their union brought about the closure of the former which has since been converted into a private house,

Primitive Methodist outing to Weymouth, 1926

'Brookside'. The 'Prims' as they were called joined the Wesleyans in what is now the Methodist Church. Undoubtedly this village was once a Methodist stronghold. In the booklet, *The Early Dorset Methodists* by Barry Biggs, one reads that a preaching house was opened in 1774 on the site of the present building and that it was probably the first in a Dorset village. A Methodist Society had been in existence for some time due to the efforts of Stephen Smith, a farmer at Forest Farm, and some members of the Broadway family, also farmers, whose very conspicuous table tomb is in front of the churchyard.

It must have been a great day on 15 September 1779 when John Wesley himself visited Motcombe to preach. Thereafter Methodism made rapid progress. In the late 1820s the Primitive Methodists, who had separated from the Wesleyans, had sufficient members to build their own chapel. In 1870 the Wesleyans erected a much larger and grander building, the present Methodist Church, in front of the original preaching house. The combined seating capacity of both chapels was over 580, whereas the Anglican Church accommodated 450, thus indicating the strength of Methodism in the village. Church attendance at the time was very poor. Lady Westminster, herself a staunch Anglican, and always solicitous for the spiritual and physical welfare of her Motcombe people, was so concerned that in 1880 she issued a letter exhorting them to come to church because, she said, it was their duty to do so and to give thanks for all the material benefits they had received, mostly provided by her.

More Motcombe Methodists

ALTHOUGH the people of Motcombe were grateful to Lady Westminster, and the noble lady was highly regarded, it was not to the Church that they went to give thanks but to the Chapel – and continued to do so. The church at that time was greatly disadvantaged. Being part of the Gillingham parish and served by curates who, though resident, were frequently changed. This arrangement ended, however, in 1883 when Motcombe became a separate parish with its own Vicar. Among Methodist personalities in times past was Mrs Mary Tuffin of Red House Farm, who for many years played a prominent role in the Primitive Chapel.

Red House Farm, Mrs Tuffin's home

Farmers who were Methodists were usually Wesleyans – such as Uriah Benjafield of Shorts Green Farm, followed by his notable son, Nathaniel, who was remembered attending chapel on Sunday mornings wearing a top hat and a frock coat. This family was among those who contributed a guinea each towards the building of the Central Hall, Westminster in 1912, and their names are recorded there on the Methodist Historical Roll.

These Benjafields were related to Frederick Benjafield whose memorial is in front of the Methodist Church. He came from Stalbridge and farmed at Frog Lane Farm.

Mention, too, must be made of Mr and Mrs George Thompson who lived at 41, The Street. Both gave years of dedicated service to the Methodist cause. George died in 1948 three years after his wife. On 20 September 1932 a special service was held in Gillingham to celebrate the union between the Primitive and Wesleyan Chapels. Motcombe Methodist Sunday School children were amongst those who received a medal to commemorate the occasion and one of these, at least, is still in existence.

The Anniversary of Motcombe Methodist Church

ON Sunday 28 June 2009 the Methodist Church celebrated their 235th anniversary. That is the anniversary when the first chapel or meeting house, as it was called, was opened in 1774. It stood on the site of the present building and was said to have been the first in a Dorset village.

The Methodist Chapel, Motcombe (formerly Wesleyan Methodist)

There was already a well established Methodist society in Motcombe at that time due to the efforts of Stephen Smith, a farmer at Little Lodge farm now Forest Farm. He was class leader and remained so for many years. He was also one of the original trustees.

Five years later on 15 September 1779 John Wesley himself came to Motcombe and preached.

In times now well in the past, but still within living memory for a few, the anniversary was, as it still is, an important occasion and was a two-day event, Sunday and a weekday when there were special services with visiting preachers from within and without the circuit. A public tea preceded the weekday service when solos were sung and also there were other forms of appropriate entertainment.

The Sunday school anniversary usually took place in July when the children, then called scholars, entertained the congregation at a special Sunday afternoon service by giving recitations and singing solos and duets. This was also a two day event.

The Sunday school teachers were then Mr and Mrs George Thompson and their brother-in-law Sydney Green.

The Primitive Methodists 'Prims' celebrated their anniversary in a similar way. They were much younger: their chapel having been built in 1828.

The Primitive Methodists and Mrs Tuffin

THE Primitive Methodist chapel in Motcombe, known as the Providence Chapel, was built in 1828, 54 years after the first Wesleyan chapel.

This came about following a visit of some Primitive Methodist missionaries in 1826, which resulted in quite a number of conversions sufficient to warrant the building of a preaching house as it was then called and, with the converts in the surrounding area, to form a Motcombe circuit with a resident minister whose home was in the thatched cottage opposite the chapel (No 40 The Street). Five of the Motcombe converts became travelling preachers, one of whom was Robert Tuffin, whose family were Wesleyan Methodists. His son, also called Robert, was brought up by his uncle and aunt, George and Mary Bartley of Red House Farm. When they died he inherited the farm and later became the owner of the Wilton Hotel in London. He married Mary Spinney, whose father was one of the three Motcombe blacksmiths at that time. The Spinneys were all staunch 'Prims'. Throughout her long life Mary Tuffin was synonymous with the Motcombe 'Prims'. She was

Primitive Methodist gathering at Red House, about 1910

their chief benefactor, contributing generously to the upkeep of the chapel, providing the Sunday school children with presents and outings and the adults with parties. Every Sunday some of the Sunday school children were invited to tea at Red House and once a year there was a party when a local band would be in attendance. When her husband died in 1914, she took over the farm and the hotel.

The various Methodist sects were re-united in 1932. The decision was then made to close the Providence chapel and use the Wesleyan chapel, which had been rebuilt in 1870. But this did not happen in Mrs Tuffin's lifetime (perhaps they did not dare!). However she died three years later aged 89. There was no room left in the little graveyard at the east end of the chapel where some of her relatives are buried. Consequently she had to be buried in the churchyard. Not long after her death the chapel, which had served Motcombe's Primitive Methodists for over a century, was converted into a private house and is now called 'Brookside'

Lord Stalbridge's Other Memorial

As well as the village hall, Lord Stalbridge has another memorial in Motcombe. It is the stained glass window above the side altar in the church.

The three figures depicted are, from left to right, Abraham representing Faith, St. Michael representing Justice and David representing Fortitude. At the foot of the window is the inscription: 'They that sow in tears shall reap in joy'.

There are several symbolic emblems and the Stalbridge coat of arms can be seen at the bottom of the central light.

The window was erected by his Lordship's tenants on the Motcombe and Stalbridge estates. The inscription on the tablet below the window reads: – 'To the Glory of God and in Fond Memory of Richard de Aquila First Baron Stalbridge who died 18 May 1912, this Window and Tablet are here placed by his Lordship's Tenantry'.

The unveiling ceremony was performed by the Earl of Shaftesbury on 18 July 1914. His wife, formerly Lady Sibell Grosvenor, was Lord Stalbridge's great niece.

The list of subscribers does not appear to have survived, unlike that of the memorial hall where the list shows that most of the cost was met by large donations from members of the Grosvenor family, including the Duke of Westminster, and the Hamilton-Stubbers (Lady Stalbridge's relations). Also a substantial contribution from the London & North Western Railway Company of which Lord Stalbridge was a former chairman.

Chapel Harvest Festival Sale in Pre-War Days

IN pre-war days the produce collected by both church and chapel for their respective harvest festivals was afterwards sold by auction.

The chapel sale took place in the room at the rear of the building, then called the schoolroom.

The produce was auctioned by Spencer Burden, better known as Spenny Burden. He was not an auctioneer by profession, but was employed at Prideaux's Motcombe factory as an outride [a rep.].

Spenny liked the bidding to be brisk, so if anyone made a last minute bid the offender would receive a fierce glare and the terse comment 'Can't dwell' adding that they would be there all night unless they got a move on.

On occasions when several bids of the same amount were made the comment would be 'All over the place' which was sometimes repeated two or three times.

Fred Stacey, the chapel caretaker, acted as auctioneer's assistant and held up the lots for all to see. For items such as potatoes he would call out the quantity such as 'About dree [three] peck'.

When a request was made for a particular item to be auctioned next, Fred, in order to make sure it was the correct one, would point to it and enquire using the good old Dorset dialect word 'Theasum? ', [This one].

Older children, who were lucky enough to have a penny or perhaps two, would hope to buy a few apples or pears but for a penny it would be the only bid. Sometimes an adult would allow you to bid for them and that was really good fun.

It would be dark when the sale ended. There were no street lights then and hardly any cars so it was all very peaceful and quiet. We made our way home in the darkness and silence feeling quite secure; knowing that any footsteps we heard would be those of someone we knew as we all knew one another in Motcombe in those days.

7
Significant Dates in Motcombe's History

1318   The first vicar of Gillingham was instituted with a stipulation that a house be made available at Motcombe for the priest officiating in the chapel there. Motcombe was then part of the ecclesiastical parish of Gillingham.

1625   Charles I gave orders that the Forest of Gillingham should be disafforested and enclosed. Motcombe was included in the Forest.

1632   Charles I sold the Manor of Gillingham to the Earl of Elgin. Motcombe belonged to the Manor.

1642   Henry Whitaker bought Motcombe House, then known as 'Palmers Place'.

1646   The parishioners of Motcombe successfully petitioned the Dorset Standing Committee to become a separate ecclesiastical parish but this was short lived; with the Restoration of the Monarchy in 1660, Motcombe had to revert to its former status.

1660   Sir Edward Nicholas, Secretary of State, bought Gillingham Manor. His residence was at Paynes Place.

1768   Gillingham Manor was sold and bought by William Sykes. His residence was at Pensbury House.

About 1774   A Motcombe Chapel was built. It stood on the same site as the present building.

1779   John Wesley preached at Motcombe.

1816 William Whitaker, the last of that family, died at Palmers Place.

1821 The second Earl Grosvenor, who later became the first Marquess of Westminster, purchased Gillingham Manor.

1825 Earl Grosvenor purchased the Motcombe estate of about eight hundred acres from Whitaker's trustees. Palmers Place was now called Motcombe House.

About 1825 Earl Grosvenor undertook an extensive programme of improvements and alterations to his farms and land at Motcombe and Gillingham.

1828 The Primitive Methodist chapel built. Now a private residence called 'Brookside'.

1831 The Marquisate of Westminster created with Earl Grosvenor as the first Marquess. His eldest son, Richard, succeeded him as Earl Grosvenor.

1832 Motcombe House became the home of the Earl and Countess Grosvenor. The Rev. Henry Deane appointed Vicar of Gillingham; a post he held for 50 years. Motcombe was still part of his parish and was served by a non-resident curate.

1838 The road from the church to the junction with the Gillingham road built. Now known as 'Turnpike Road'.

1839 Motcombe School and schoolhouse completed. Elizabeth Perry, who had trained at the National School in Westminster, was appointed first teacher.

1845 Death of the first Marquess of Westminster. Earl Grosvenor succeeded to the title.

1846 Motcombe church pulled down and rebuilt on the same site.

1847 The new church consecrated.

Between 1850 – 1870 Motcombe extensively rebuilt by the second Marquess of Westminster. Several farms and many of the present houses date from this period.

1859 A night school was started with Lord and Lady Westminster, their youngest daughter, Lady Theodora Grosvenor, and the Rev. Rogers (the curate) as teachers. The railway opened between Salisbury and Gillingham.

1860 A house built for the curate, now part of 'The Old Rectory'.

1869 Death of the second Marquess of Westminster. His widow inherited the Motcombe estate and the Manor of Gillingham for her lifetime.

1871 A new and bigger Wesleyan Methodist chapel was opened on the same site as the old one. An improved water supply was provided by Lady Westminster. A reservoir holding 40,000 gallons was built at Bittles Green and taps were installed at convenient places in the village. Water was also piped to the outlying farms.

1874 Due to an increase in numbers, Lady Westminster provided a new school building for the boys.

1877 The marriage of Lady Theodora Grosvenor to Thomas Merthyr Guest took place in the church. In Motcombe and Shaftesbury there were big celebrations.

1879 Charles Prideaux, later proprietor of Motcombe factory, started business trading in dairy produce.

1883 Motcombe, with Enmore Green, became a separate ecclesiastical parish with the Rev .Canon John Smith as the first vicar.

1887 A new ring of bells was installed to celebrate Queen Victoria's Golden Jubilee. They rang for the first time on Lady Westminster's ninetieth birthday.

1891 Death of Lady Westminster at the age of ninety-four. The Mayor and Corporation of Shaftesbury led the funeral procession from Motcombe to the church. Over three thousand people lined the route near the church. Her son, Lord Stalbridge, inherited the Motcombe estate and the Lordship of the Gillingham Manor.

1893 – 1895 Old Motcombe House was pulled down and a new mansion built. Now Port Regis School.

1893 Motcombe Nursing Association and the Slate and Loan Club were formed.

1894 The Parish Council was formed with eleven elected councilors.

1898 The first Bonfire Night Carnival took place. The procession was headed by Motcombe School's fife and drum band followed by decorated horse-drawn floats.

1899 Outbreak of the Boer War. Motcombe members of the Dorset Imperial Yeomanry called up.

1900 Motcombe Cricket Club formed. There had previously been a Motcombe House cricket team.

1901 Wedding of Hon. Blanche Grosvenor, second daughter of the first Baron Stalbridge, and Captain James Holford in Motcombe church. Big celebrations in the village.

1902 The Coronation of Edward VII celebrated with a tea, sports and fireworks. Each schoolchild received a mug.

1903 New extension to the churchyard consecrated.

1907 New choir stalls, pulpit and organ in the church dedicated by the Bishop of Salisbury.

1911 The Coronation of George V celebrated in the same manner as Edward VII.

1912 Death of first Baron Stalbridge. His eldest son, Hugh, succeeded to the title.

1914 The second Baron Stalbridge, with his wife and son, took up residence at Motcombe House. The village decorated with flags and streamers for the occasion. Motcombe Scout group formed by Lady Stalbridge. Outbreak of the Great War. Private Charles Arnold of the 6th Dragoon Guards the first casualty. He was wounded at the Battle of Mons.

1915 Memorial services held for Sgt. Gibbons and Captain the Hon. Richard Grosvenor. Both killed in action.

1918 End of the Great War. Thirty-one men from the parish gave their lives. Twelve, from Motcombe, and nineteen from Enmore Green and Sherborne Causeway.

1920 The War Memorial was unveiled by Lady Stalbridge and dedicated by the Bishop of Salisbury.

1921 The Parochial Church Council came into being.

1924 The inaugural concert of Motcombe Choral Society took place in the schoolroom.

1925 Sale of the Motcombe estate. Lord and Lady Stalbridge left the village. Charles Prideaux, proprietor of Motcombe factory, now becomes the principal personage. He built houses in Shorts Green Lane for his workers and also bought some of the estate houses and farms.

1926 Lord Stalbridge gave the school to the church authorities and the recreation ground to the village.

1928 The Memorial Hall was officially opened.

1929 Charles Prideaux bought Motcombe House which had been threatened with demolition.

1930 Motcombe Women's Institute was formed. Death of the Hon. Hugh Raufe Grosvenor, aged 25, as the result of a flying accident. He was Lord Stalbridge's son and heir to the title.

1931 The first village fete and flower show was held. It was a great success and £80 profit was made.

1932 Union of the Wesleyan and Primitive Methodists. The two Motcombe chapels continued to operate separately until 1936, when the Primitive Methodist chapel was closed.

1933 Despite strong protests, Enmore Green, hitherto part of the parish of Motcombe, was incorporated into the Borough of Shaftesbury. Sale of the remainder of the Motcombe estate which included the Post Office (now The Old Post House) and six houses. Electricity was installed in many homes in the village but some, mainly the elderly, preferred to retain their oil lamps and candles.

1935 Celebrations for the Silver Jubilee of King George V and Queen Mary took place with a church service followed by a tea for everyone and sports for the children ending with a dance in the evening. The school children listened to the King's speech in the Memorial Hall. The girls received a Jubilee cup and saucer and the boys a mug.

1936 The Jubilee Corner (a garden) was opened. A house now stands on the site.

1937 The Coronation of King George VI was celebrated in much the same way as the Jubilee in 1935, except that the children received a beaker and a plate.

1939 Outbreak of the Second World War. Many evacuees arrived in the village but most of the women with small children soon returned to London preferring to face Hitler's bombs rather than live in Motcombe. A new secondary school was opened at Shaftesbury. Motcombe children between the ages of 11-14 went by a school bus every day to attend this school.

1940 Death of Charles Prideaux at The Grange aged 87. He was the principal property owner in the village and the majority of Motcombe's working population was employed at his factory.

Dates and Datestones

MOTCOMBE people whose homes were once Westminster cottages know the age of their property, because, with one or two exceptions, they all have date stones. Westminster cottages are, by way of explanation, those built by the second Marquess of Westminster, mainly in the 1850s and 60s to provide the labouring classes, as they were then called, with better homes.

But date stones can sometimes be misleading and the former turnpike house, now numbers 3 and 4 Turnpike Cottages, is a good example. It was first built between 1837 and 1838, when the old road across Motcombe Park was stopped and the present one via the Church and Manor Farm was constructed. The old turnpike house and gate were situated near the main entrance to Port Regis School by Latchmore Pond.

The new turnpike survived for less than thirty years; when the Shaftesbury and Sherborne Turnpike Trust was abolished in 1865 it was no longer required. In the following year it was converted into a semi-detached house and another storey added. The year 1866, on the date stone, therefore denotes the date of the conversion, not when it was originally built.

The old workhouse, now numbers 18 to 21 Motcombe, does not favour us with a date, but it was built in 1806, although it appears to be older. This is because the stone used in its construction had come from an old house called 'Thornhills' which stood near Frog Lane Farm. It had been the home of the Wyke (or Wykes) family for several generations; minor gentry who had their own chapel in the old Motcombe Church. Frances Wyke was the founder of one of the three former Motcombe Charities.

Of the Motcombe farms to be rebuilt by the Marquess of Westminster, Frog Lane Farm, was the last and the only one not to have a date. It was completed in 1868, a year before his Lordship's death on the last day of October 1869.

8

In the Times of the Royal Manor and Forest

Fly Tipping, Enforcement Orders, Encroachments and Thieves

THE Manor and Forest Court Rolls of Gillingham show that our ancestors were familiar with some of the problems that we experience today. For example:

Fly Tipping – 19 April 1572

The inhabitants of Shaston bring carrion and dunge and deposit it in the tithing of Motcombe at a place called Nettlebedde near the Queen's highway to the great nuisance of the Queen's soldiers. It is ordered that they reform and do not continue this nuisance on pain of 6s 8d for anyone caught doing it.

Nettlebedde is at the bottom of Shaftesbury Hill on the sharp bend where one turns right for Motcombe near Pensbury House. It is still called Nettlebed Corner, at least by the older generation, but it appears to be becoming another forgotten place name. This area is no longer in the civil parish of Motcombe having been incorporated into the Borough of Shaftesbury along with Enmore Green in 1933.

An Enforcement Order – 10 June 1572

The tithing man of Motcombe presents that John Jaques has built a pyggestie (pigsty) on land which is exposed to the bedroom of William Senior to the great nuisance of the said William and the said John is ordered to remove it before the next court on pain of 6s 8d.

Boundary encroachments were always coming up at the court. The offenders were usually ordered to go back to the original boundaries.

Thieves – 19 April 1572
John Swyfte of Motcombe labourer is a common thief not in the service of anyone and not married. Therefore the tithing man is ordered to place the said John in custody before the next court so he may receive justice.

So it seems that it has all happened before.

A Threatened Stabbing in Motcombe Churchyard

F ORTUNATELY the above incident did not occur recently, but in 1576 when it was recorded in the court rolls of the Royal Manor and Forest of Gillingham that:

> Edmund Hilgrove uttered contumacious words to the Constable of Motcombe and the Constable wished to arrest him in the churchyard at Motcombe but the said Edmund drew his sword from its scabbard and threatened to stab him against the Queen's peace. Therefore the Constable pleads with the inhabitants to help him arrest the said Edmund. And his sword is forfeit and the bailiff must render it to the Queen.

The dictionary definition of contumacious is to oppose rightful authority and be wilfully disobedient to the orders of a court. This definition is borne out in an earlier entry which states that 'Edmund Hilgrove has not received communion for the space of one year past and therefore complaint is made according to the statute.' The outcome was that he was fined 12d and the money went to the poor.

On the subject of the poor a good example of naming and shaming occurs in 1571 when the rolls reveal that the Rector and Vicar of Gillingham were ordered to pay a portion for the maintenance of the poor adding that they had not done enough for the past twenty-four years to the great harm of the poor. Motcombe was then included in the ecclesiastical parish of Gillingham and continued to be so until 1883.

Reverting to the year 1576 a certain John Mathew had to come to the court as a supplicant, that is saying sorry and asking forgiveness because he had been caught stealing apples from Giles Hussey's orchard at Motcombe after the sun had set. John was probably a lad hence the nature of the punishment.

Motcombe's Stocks and Neighbour Problems

MOTCOMBE was once a tithing, that is a division or part of the Royal Manor and Forest of Gillingham. Its inhabitants therefore were subject to the laws of the manor and forest. Offenders were brought before the manor court by the tithingman, an elected representative of the tithing, for punishment which, in the case of minor offences, could mean being placed in the stocks. An entry in the manor court rolls for 30th September 1617 serves as a good example.

> Joane Bounde of Motcombe is a common scolde and a slanderer of her neighbours upon the Sabbath daye. Ordered that the Constable or Tithingman of Motcombe set her in the stocks upon the Sabbath or festival daye in a public place with a text hand or Roman letter. This is a Scolde by the space of three hours.

The stocks had to be kept in good repair as is evident from the entry of 24th September 1691

> The tithingman presents that the stocks at Motcombe are in disrepair and must be mended by the next court on pain of 40s.

It is clear from the entry of 19 October 1620 that there were problems with the neighbours in those days too.

> It is consented to and agreed in open Courte that after the Feast of All Saints next ensuing noe Inhabitant of Motcombe shall keepe anye Duckes in the water called Church Street Water in Motcombe which hath formerly bynne a great annoyance to the neighbours upon pain of 2s 8d.

Church Street as the name implies was in the area around the church and included the present church walk.

More about Motcombe in the Times of the Manor and Forest

ALTHOUGH Joane Bounde was put in the stocks for being a 'common scolde' in 1617, five years later, in October 1622, another woman was punished differently for the same offence.

> Anne Warlland the wyffe of John Warland of Motcombe is a Common Scolde and a malicious tongued woman against her neighbours. Ordered that she be punyshed by the Constable of Motcombe in the Tumbrell three or twoe times at least before Christmas next.

A Tumbrell at that time was a stool bolted on to a wheeled platform. The offender would be paraded around in it for all to see and to ridicule and throw things at. In those days too it appears you had to be very careful whom you had living in your home. In 1595, the manor court fined William Brodway 12d 'for harbouring unknown suspicious persons in his house despite warnings from the tithingman' but in 1598 he did the right thing as did Thomas Dirdo.

> William Brodway and Thomas Dirdo come to the court and wish to build a cottage or house in Motcombe and this is agreed and it will be handed over to the Queen the Lord of the Manor.

Not everyone, however, sought permission but did not succeed in getting away with it.

> They present one cottage erected in the tithing of Motcombe in this Manor in which John Drinkwater now lives to be an encroachment and it should be handed over to the benefit of the Queen.

The court was concerned too with the safety and welfare of the inhabitants.

> 1581, Ordered that the alehouse keepers do not allow Poor Lawborers to sit tiplinge in their houses but to deliver them for their money home to their houses to helpe refresh their wyves and children.

1622, Rychard Hascall doth suffer Christian Bartlett his tenant to make fyer in an owt house where ys noe chymney very dangerous to his neighbours ordered that noe more fyer be made therein unless a chymney be built therein on pain of 10s.

9
Motcombe Miscellaneous

Glimpses of the Past: Motcombe's Allotments

A T one time there were three allotment sites in Motcombe: Brickells Plot; Lakehouse Mead and Bowers. Brickell's Plot was the smallest, about two acres. This site, now built on, was immediately south of No. 43 The Street. Lakehouse Mead, this six acre site situated behind the bungalows in Bittles Green, was popular because the stream running through provided water. Bowers, although the largest [nine acres], was inconveniently situated about half way up Motcombe Hollow on the left hand side going towards Shaftesbury.

Bittles Green, about 1906

Plot sizes were measured in lugs, the Dorset word for a rod, pole or perch which was 5½ yards in length. It is known that at least one plotholder cultivated forty lugs.

Larger gardens at home, smaller families and improved living standards between the two world wars, meant that Motcombe allotments were no longer required and were converted into agricultural land.

In a recent 'Villager' there was an article on the former allotments in Motcombe. However, there were others, although of a different nature. These were plots of land allotted to the freeholders and copyholders in the Forest of Gillingham, which included Motcombe, as compensation for loss of grazing and others rights in the Forest following the disafforestation in about 1624.

Although field names are now unfortunately falling into disuse, at least three fields can still be identified as originally being allotted land. Two at North End Farm called 'Higher Allotment' and 'Lower Allotment' and one at East Coppleridge Farm called 'Allotment'. Church Farm used to be called Allotment Farm because several of its fields were allotment land including sixteen acres allotted to the poor of Motcombe at the time of the disafforestation; the rent from which provided the income for the former Allotment Lands Charity.

The Poet and the Lady and the Little Book on Motcombe

IN a letter to Lady Theodora Guest dated 14th May 1883, the Rev. William Barnes, the Dorset poet, refers to her little book on Motcombe and says that he is much pleased with it. Lady Theodora Guest née Grosvenor was the youngest of the thirteen children of Richard, second Marquess of Westminster. She was born in 1840 and until her marriage in 1877 had spent most of her life at Motcombe House near Shaftesbury, her father's Dorset seat.

Her husband was Thomas Merthyr Guest, second son of Sir Josiah John Guest, the ironmaster, whose residence was at Canford Manor near Wimborne. Her home after her marriage was at Inwood House in the parish of Henstridge on the Dorset-Somerset border and only about ten miles from her beloved Motcombe. Her connection with her native village was still maintained however, as she and her husband used to spend the summers with her widowed mother at Motcombe House until the latter's death in 1891.

Her love for her native home and the surrounding countryside where she claimed to know every field and lane, inspired her to write 'the little book on Motcombe' with the title *Motcombe Past and Present* and a sub-title 'being a slight sketch of some of the points of interest in its immediate neighbourhood'. It covers other places as far as Fonthill to the east and Stalbridge and Bagber, where William Barnes was born, to the west, nearly all of which were the property of her father, the Marquess, who was a large landowner in that area.

The first edition, published by C. Bastable of Shaftesbury, appeared in 1867. There were only 150 copies and were soon all sold, leading to a second edition in the following year. These two editions were illustrated with five sketches, by the author, of buildings including Motcombe House, mentioned in the book. There was a third and final edition in 1873 but without the illustrations. Barnes was correct in describing it as a little book for it measured approximately six and a half inches in length and four in width. It is probably one of the earliest histories of a Dorset village and is, in booksellers' parlance, scarce. Therefore, whenever a copy does appear in their catalogues it commands a good price. There were quite a number of presentation copies, some of which are now in the possession of the descendants of the recipients.

In his letter the poet also refers to three books of his poems which it would appear Lady Theodora had asked him to sign, saying that he had taken pleasure in doing so and was pleased to know that she thinks them worthy of her bookshelf. In addition to his signature each book has an inscription in verse. The first reads:

> Long sing thou little book with Dorset voice,
> So honor'd by a noble Lady's choice.

The second has:

> Long may'st thou keep o honor'd book the shelf
> Of her who kindly marked thee for herself.

The third is rather melancholy:

> O may those eyes for which is written here
> My name, be aye answered by a tear.

The reason for the sad tone of this dedication is not known.

The poet died in 1886 at the age of 85. The Lady lived at Inwood

House until her death in 1924 aged 83. She maintained her connection with Motcombe until the end.

More about the Railway

ALTHOUGH Gillingham celebrated the opening of the railway on 2nd May 1859, the next station up the line, Semley, did not and that is understandable; for it was situated at a considerable distance from the village near the junction with the A350 Shaftesbury to Warminster road. It was built there primarily for the benefit of Shaftesbury rather than Semley, as for obvious reasons, this hilltop town could not have a station. So Semley was referred to as 'our station'.

From the date of the opening a horse drawn omnibus from the Grosvenor Hotel met the trains at Semley and in later years it was replaced by a motorbus. Semley was also the station for Motcombe but more than fifty years were to elapse before there was any form of hired transport to and from the station. Intending rail passengers had to make their own way there, either by some form of horse conveyance or on foot. One way was to walk along the railway track but, although this was trespassing, it was often done particularly by servicemen in the two world wars.

Since Motcombe was denied a station or even a halt, milk and other goods from Prideaux's factory had to be taken to Semley station by horse and cart and after the arrival of motorised transport, by lorry. About the time of the First World War, William Stacey and his son Tom, of Barn House, Motcombe, who were in business as dealers in dairy produce, fruit and vegetables, began a hire service to the stations and elsewhere at first by waggonette or trap and shortly after the war by motor car. Their advertisement in a trade directory read 'Conveyance. W L Stacey and Son will meet trains with motor car by appointment'

During the course of time and with improved rail services Gillingham began to be used more, especially for travel down the line and also because some fast up trains to London stopped there thus avoiding a change at Salisbury.

Wells and Water

THE brooks that run through Motcombe were formerly the main source of it's water supply. Hence the reason why, despite the risk of flooding, most of the houses in the lower part of the village are situated close to the brooks for easy access to the water, which was dipped up when required into stone pitchers and carried into the houses. Wells were the other source of supply; generally for those living at a distance from the brooks.

The brooks originated from springs in the nearby hills. Although pure spring water it could become contaminated, but fortunately there are no recorded cases of any waterborne diseases affecting Motcombe. This danger was reduced in about 1860 when the Marquess of Westminster, The Lord of the Manor, had the water from some of the springs channeled into pipes and bought down to public pumps stationed at convenient sites through the village.

In 1871, his widow, Lady Westminster, greatly improved the system when a reservoir holding 40,000 gallons was built at Bittles Green from whence the water was piped to all the farms and to within easy reach of each house. Lady Westminster herself was present when the water was turned on for the first time at Dunedge Lodge Farm.

Cricket in Motcombe

MOTCOMBE Cricket Club was formed in 1900 but before that, there had been a Motcombe House Cricket Club. Very little information about this club exists, however it is known that it was in existence in the 1860s and consisted mainly of employees on the Motcombe estate

Motcombe cricket team, about 1928

excluding the labourers. The curate of Motcombe, The Rev. Oldfield, also played as well as two tenant farmers.

Matches were not held on a regular basis and took place on a weekday evening in the cricket field, which was one of the fields belonging to Church Farm or Allotment Farm as it was then called. It is located at the end of the pathway by the old workhouse. There was a pavilion here where Lord and Lady Westminster and their daughter Lady Theodora Grosvenor would be seated when they came down from Motcombe House to support their team.

Motcombe Cricket Club was a properly constituted body. Spencer (Spenny) Burden was the first secretary and continued to be so for over fifty years. Another long serving member was Charley Clark who, when too old to play, continued as an umpire. The club was at its peak during the inter-war years. In the 1920s the vicar, The Rev. King, was the captain; he was succeeded by Frank Littlecot. A photograph taken in about 1928 of the team, show all, except one to be living in Motcombe.

During the war several of the members were called up but matches continued. In the post war years there have been a couple of periods when the club has not been functioning but it is pleasing to know that it is again fully operational with regular fixtures.

Motcombe Boy Scouts, 1914–1939

Motcombe scout troop 1918

MOTCOMBE's first scout troop was formed in 1914 by Lady Stalbridge, wife of the second Baron Stalbridge. She was the president. David Farmer, the electrician at Motcombe House, was the scoutmaster and Cyril Adams, of Church Farm, was the assistant scoutmaster. There was a cub pack too run by Mrs Bourne, the head gardener's wife. Lord Stalbridge's only son and heir, the Hon. Hugh Raufe Grosvenor, was also a keen scout member. David Farmer started a bugle band which on one recorded occasion played at Semley fête.

Every year when the scouts went to camp, the farmers and other employers were requested by Lady Stalbridge to give any scout employed by them permission to attend. The Stalbridges left Motcombe in 1925, by that time, Colonel Nixon, Lady Stalbridge's brother, had already taken over as scoutmaster. However when he left in 1927 no one could be found to replace him so Motcombe's scout troop had to be disbanded.

In about 1936 a new troop and a cub pack were started by Mr Cogswell, who lived at Haines Farm (now Nods Fold) where meetings took place. It was on a more modest scale than the first troop and was of short duration as, with the advent of the Second World War, Motcombe scouts were again disbanded.

Motcombe's War Memorial

AS is customary on Remembrance Sunday, wreaths will be placed on the War Memorial as a tribute to those who fell in the two world wars. The Memorial was unveiled by Lady Stalbridge, then dedicated by the Bishop of Salisbury, on 20th May 1920, to the memory of the thirty-one men from the parish of Motcombe and Enmore Green, including Sherborne Causeway, who had sacrificed their lives in the 1914-1918 war. Nineteen were from Enmore Green and twelve from Motcombe, amongst whom was Lord Stalbridge's youngest brother; Captain the Hon. Richard Grosvenor M.C.

Enmore Green, which had suffered disproportionately in numbers felt they should have their own memorial there as well. This took the form of an electric street lamp inscribed with the names on a brass plaque.

It was not until 1985 that the names of the five Motcombe men who lost their lives in World War Two were added to the memorial when there was a special ceremony on Remembrance Sunday of that year to mark the occasion. Those from Enmore Green were, however, not included because in 1933 it had been incorporated into the Borough of Shaftesbury.

War memorial dedication

Tom Putt

Tom Putt is a variety of apple named after the person who raised it. It is fairly large in size and red in colour and was once widely grown in this area, primarily because it was good for cider making.

Years ago, but just within living memory, cider was a favourite drink and consequently Motcombe then abounded in apple orchards which were a pretty sight in springtime when the trees were in blossom. Most of the cider made was for home consumption although, at one time, it was produced at Motcombe's factory. The farmers usually had their own press as did other cider makers; but for those who did not possess one they could be borrowed or hired. Like wine, there were good years and not so good years. Some took great pride in the cider they produced. There was an art in making it and a few trade secrets.

Some other local varieties were; Cadburys, used mainly for cider. Profits, whose full name is Poor Man's Profit, this was a cooking apple. Mother Romseys and the Orange Apple both eating apples but were used too in cider making to sweeten it.

In winter, cider was often warmed before drinking. It was poured into a jug which was then covered and placed in the hearth. This practice is mentioned by the Dorset Poet, William Barnes, in his poem 'Praise O'Dorset'.

There are still a very few old trees of the varieties mentioned in Motcombe but their days are numbered. However both Tom Putt and Profits are thriving at the Brogdale Trust in Kent along with about 2300 other apple varieties and the others are probably there too, but under a different name.

Blackthorn Winter, Shaftesbury Rain etc.

A BLACKTHORN winter is defined as a spell of wintry weather in spring when the blackthorn is in bloom. The white flowers of this shrub appear before the leaves and its fruit is the sloe or snag in the Dorset dialect.

In the year 2008 there certainly was a blackthorn winter with snow and frost in April when the blackthorn was in full bloom. Fortunately this term is still known and used by the older generation not only locally but over quite a wide area. Whereas 'Shaftesbury rain', on the other hand was much more localised. In fact it is no longer used or known. But twenty years ago there was some correspondence in the *Western Gazette* instigated by the writer of this article which revealed that 'Shaftesbury rain' was remembered particularly by some living on the Somerset–Dorset border. It has been described as rain of twenty-four hours or more in duration with the wind in the South East.

In years gone by, Motcombe people used to say that when Shaftesbury town hall clock could be heard striking it was a sure sign of rain but when Semley church bells were heard it was a sign of fine weather.

Two Dorset dialect words remembered are 'Lippen' meaning rainy. The writer's father used to say that a lippen May was best for the garden. The second is a 'scud'. This is a light shower and was still in use a few years ago by one or two of the 'wold volk' in the village.

Old Testament First Names

OLD Testament names were popular in the last century for boys and Motcombe had its share. As well as Meshach Moore, the blacksmith, the following are also remembered: Nehemiah Arnold, understandably called 'Nemy' for short, worked at the factory until he was well over eighty and lived with Mr and Mrs Jack Lear at 48, The Street. Levi Clark did not like his first name and was called Jack as his second name was John. He worked at the factory for 55 years and lived

Church Walk, about 1906

at No. 17, Motcombe. There were two Eli's. Eli Miles worked in the butter department at the factory; Eli Stacev was an estate worker and during the war was an A.R.P. warden. Both lived in Shorts Green Lane. Lot Pitman was a gamekeeper on the estate and in retirement lived in the cottage at the end of New Lane. Samuel Smart, better known as 'Sammy', was a gardener at Motcombe House. He was working there as a young man in Lady Westminster's time and lived all his life at 5, Church Walk.

Life in Motcombe in Hard Winters Years Ago

THE winter of 2010, which was unusually cold, with much more snow and ice, has brought back memories of similar winters years ago in Motcombe in the present writer's boyhood days.

Like most villages at that time Motcombe was almost self-contained, as day-to-day requirements could be obtained from the shops and the factory without having to go to Shaftesbury or Gillingham, a great blessing in bad weather. In addition Motcombe was also well served by tradesmen who came regularly once or twice a week. In those days the horse and van was still much in evidence.

For the very few car owners a journey outside the village to the nearest petrol pumps was necessary, but paraffin could be bought from Shutes, later Haydens, (now the present village store), for the oil lamps before electricity came. Although there were at least two tradesmen with a Motcombe round who sold paraffin.

Coal, another necessity, was supplied by merchants from Shaftesbury and Gillingham so it was advisable to keep well stocked up lest weather conditions prevented deliveries.

This was particularly so in the case of Shaftesbury tradesmen because, when there was deep snow, Puckmore Hollow, to give it the correct name, could be blocked at the top by drifts several feet deep. Children going to Shaftesbury schools and people working in the town would also be severely affected.

To prevent skidding cars and other motorised transport had chains on their wheels and the horses had frost nails in their shoes or sacking over their hooves. Fortunately most of the people employed at the factory lived in the village. The few who did not, had to walk to work and were put up at homes in the village until conditions improved enabling them to return home each day. The school kept open although children living at a distance often could not get there. On arrival the pupils would crowd round the coke burning 'Tortoise' stove to warm up.

The ice storm during the hard winter of 1939/40 caused much havoc, the telegraph wires on the poles through the village came down due to the weight of the ice, and many trees lost branches. The small lake near Motcombe House was frozen hard permitting skating and sliding. The pavements and parts of Motcombe Street were cleared of snow and ice by the two resident roadmen Bob Wareham and Albert Viney.

In those days there was not the fuss made about the weather as there is today, we just 'kept calm and carried on'.

Bibliography

Ash, J., *Victorian vicar: the story of Henry Deane*. Gillingham, 1982
Ash, J., *West Stour in Dorset*. Sherborne, 1980
Baxter, L., *The life of William Barnes*, London, 1887
Biggs, B. J., *The Wesleys and the early Dorset Methodists*. Gillingham, 1987
Evans, M., *The place of the rural blacksmith in parish life.1500-1900*. Taunton 1998
Francis, C., *St.James's Church, Shaftesbury: a brief guide*
Grosvenor, Lady T., *Motcombe past and present*, 1st, 2nd, 3rd eds. Shaftesbury, 1867,1868, 1873
Grosvenor, Lady T., *Simple thoughts on Bible truths*. London, 1873
Guest, R and John, A., *Lady Charlotte: a biography of the nineteenth century*. London, 1989
Guest, Lady T., *A round trip in North America*. London, 1895
Hutchins, Rev. J., *The history and antiquities of the county of Dorset*, 3rd ed, London, 1861- 4
Huxley,E., *Nellie: letters from Africa*. London, 1973
Huxley, G., *Lady Elizabeth and the Grosvenors*. London, 1965
Huxley, G., *Victorian duke*. London, 1967
Kerr, B., *Bound to the soil: a social history of Dorset*. London, 1968
Reeves, J. M., *From Dorset farm to Ohio factory*. U.S.A., 1992
Sawyer. R., *Nadder: tales of a Wiltshire valley*. East Knoyle, 2006
Shaftesbury Historical Society., *A short history of the Westminster Memorial Hospital, Shaftesbury, Dorset, 1871-1971*
Stalbridge, Lady G., *H.R.G.: a memoir of Hugh Raufe Grosvenor*
Wagner, A.F.H.V., *The Church of St. Mary the Virgin, Gillingham*. Gillingham, 1956

Newspapers

Bideford Weekly Gazette
Dorset County Chronicle
Faringdon Advertiser
Register News – Pictorial

Salisbury and Winchester Journal
Shaftesbury Gazette
Three Shires Advertiser
Sunday Express
The Times
Western Gazette

Periodicals and Magazines

Agricultural World
The Builder
Country Life
The Graphic
St. James's Church, Shaftesbury, Magazine

Reference Books

Burke's Landed Gentry
The Clergy Guide
The Clergy List
Crockford's Clerical Directory
Debrett's Illustrated Peerage
Kelly's Directories of Dorsetshire

Census Returns for Motcombe and West Knoyle
Motcombe Parish Registers

Acknowledgements.

I AM grateful to all those who, over the course of many years, have provided me with photographs, which have been published in my articles in the *Dorset Year Book* and now appear in this book.

I am especially grateful to Count Richard de Pelet for allowing me access to the archives at Inwood House. Also all those who have willingly shared their knowledge on various subjects with me.

My thanks go to Barrie Pictures, for their consent to publish photographs from their collection and to the governors of Motcombe School for their permission to read and quote from the early log books. With special thanks to Mrs Jenny Lucas for her kind assistance on the more recent history of the school.

I am indebted to Mr Jay M Reeves, co-author with the late Kathryn Hess and Thomas Hamilton of *From Dorset Farm to Ohio Factory* which enabled me to write my article on the Reeves family.

My thanks are also due to the archivists at The Eaton Estate office and the Dorset History Centre.

I must also mention Professor Diana Coben for kindly reading my articles and for her helpful suggestions.

I much appreciate the help Dr John Chandler has given me in the preparation of this book.

And finally Valerie, my wife, for all the photocopying, and Elizabeth, my daughter, for typing and later computerising my articles and deciphering my ever deteriorating handwriting.